ON THE BRINK

ON THE BRINK

A Korean Diplomat's Journey for Peace

Han SungJoo

Hannam Policy Institute (IpsiKor)

Ollim

FIRST EDITION

Designed by Jin Hyelee

Han SungJoo
ON THE BRINK: A Korean Diplomat's Journey for Peace
ISBN 979-11-6262-003-8 03340
CIP 2018025820

Dedicated to, and in memory of, my mentors, colleagues and friends, and their legacy:

Prof. Robert A. Scalapino, Prof. John T. Holden, George E. Jonas, Don Oberdorfer (United States), Qian Qichen(China), Shimon Peres(Israel), Boutros Boutros-Ghali(Egypt), Tadashi Yamamoto(Japan), Kim Jun-yop, Kim Kyung-won, Hyun Hong-choo, and Park Shin-il, of Korea, and Kim Jae-ik, my brother-in-law.

Contents

Chapter 1 Growing up

Chapter 2 Preparing a Career

Chapter 3 A Young Minister

Chapter 4 Ambassador in Washington

Chapter 5 A Civilian Diplomat in a Multilateral World

Chapter 6 A Grand Strategy for South Korea?

Acknowledgments

This book is intended to record how I became interested in diplomacy as a young man, how I was involved in it in an official capacity and as a civilian, what I think I learned and accomplished through these experiences, and what I think I should have done better. Thus, it is neither a scientific book nor a travelogue.

I have already written a memoir, in my native language, Korean. This book, which is not a simple translation of the earlier book, but its trimmed version, is intended to help my friends, colleagues and family members to gain a better understanding of Korea as a country, the Korean people, myself as a person, and the diplomatic challenges and opportunities that Korea faces now and in the future.

In writing this book, indeed in living my diplomatic life, which this book is about, I am indebted to numerous individuals—particularly mentors, colleagues, friends and students—who helped me and guided me in my diplomatic journey. Unfortunately, there are a few among them who have passed away and therefore to whom I will not be able to present this book and pay respect except by way of mentioning their names in print. There are simply too many individuals whom I have to thank and who are still actively engaged in diplomatic work to be able to mention their names.

For the publication of this book, I am indebted to the excellent editorial help of Ben Forney, Lisa Collins, and Anne Feder Lee. I am also thankful to Professor Gil Rozman, Professor Lee Shin-wha, Ambassador Kim Jae-Bum and Jean Lee, who read parts or all of the manuscript and contributed to its improvement. Mr. Lee Sung-Soo, president of Ollim, has been instrumental in producing a handsome book in what I consider to be a record time.

My deepest thanks are due to my wife Song-mi, who patiently bore the burden of revising parts of the manuscript while being busily engaged in finishing her own book on Korean art. This book is a present to her, our son Charles Sungwon, daughter-in-law Susan Mariko Kobayashi, and their children Mina and Dylan.

There is one particular person who has helped me to sustain my motivation to complete the manuscript for this book. Billy Kwon, a nephew of my wife's, was born in the United States where he has lived all of his life. Nonetheless, he has maintained a strong interest in and love of his parents' country, Korea. While I was writing, I had Billy in mind as an ardent reader of my memoir in English when it is published. Therefore, this book is also a gift to him as well.

This is to say that the main readers of this book I have in mind and those whom I would like to attract are foreign friends and colleagues of Korea as well as the second, third and fourth generations of Koreans who grew up and/or live abroad.If they find this book interesting and useful in getting closer to Korea, I will feel that my self-designated mission has been accomplished.

August, 2018

Han SungJoo

Author's Note

This is my second try with my "memoir." The first one, written in Korean, was published in 2017. Obviously, it was mainly for Korean readers, and thus many of my friends who do not have a strong enough command of the Korean language could not read it. Even some of my immediate family members, who were born and raised in the United States, could not read it. I wanted to amend this situation. In doing so, I did not simply translate the earlier Korean version into English. Instead, I shortened it, made it more concise, and added more explanations where needed. Hopefully this will make the book leaner, more readable, and even more informative for the reader of the English version.

14

Preface

I served as a college professor of international relations for nearly fifty years. But more than half of my life has been devoted to the service of diplomacy—teaching, researching, and practicing it. I did it both in an official capacity and as a civilian.

I still do not know what led former president Kim Young-sam to appoint me as his first foreign minister. I did not campaign for him. Neither did I serve as an expert advisor to his campaign before his election. When I was a graduate student at Berkeley, I once served (by pure chance) as Mr. Kim's interpreter at a Stanford University lecture he gave in 1968. It was the time of President Park Chung-hee's high-dictatorship (*yushin*) period, and Mr. Kim was in the political wilderness. Since then, I had seen him a couple of times when the American political scientist, Professor Robert A. Scalapino, whom Mr. Kim considered a good friend and who was my advisor at Berkeley, visited Seoul. I do not know, and do not think it likely, that they talked about me in my absence.

Perhaps Mr. Kim remembered my name as someone who spoke favorably about him during the heated presidential campaign of 1987-88 when he ran against candidates Roh Tae-woo and Kim Dae-jung. Mr. Roh won the presidency that year. At the time, I was well recognized in Korea as the only Asian columnist for the American news magazine,

Newsweek. But it was in a cover story for Time magazine that I claimed that, in a face-to-face contest between the "two Kims," Kim Young-sam and Kim Dae-jung, the former Kim with his conservative backing would be more "electable." Kim Young-sam construed this to mean that he would win in the forthcoming election. Kim promptly carried around on the campaign trail a copy of the *Time* magazine with my interview in it to claim that the prestigious publication had declared that he would be the winner! That is as much as I can conjecture about Mr. Kim's recognition of me.

Candidate Kim also must have had the impression that as a well-known personality in the diplomatic and intellectual circuits, I likely possessed good and extensive personal networks abroad, particularly in the United States.

Why President Roh Moo-hyun (2003-2008), who knew that I did not vote for him nor share many of his policy preferences, chose me to serve as his ambassador to Washington is even more difficult to fathom. Like many Koreans in the early 2000s, Roh was convinced that Washington had all but decided to carry out a surgical strike against North Korea's Yongbyun reactor back in 1994 during the first nuclear crisis and that the military disaster was prevented by the adroit(?) diplomatic effort of the South Korean foreign minister at the time—

meaning me! It did not matter that the Clinton administration had made no decisions regarding such plans to attack Yongbyun and that neither my intervention, nor that of President Kim Young-sam, stopped the Americans from bombing North Korea. Once a perception is planted in people's (particularly politicians') minds, it is nearly impossible to pluck out.

President Roh had another, more pragmatic, reason to appoint me as ambassador to Washington. The holdover ambassador from Roh's predecessor, Kim Dae-Jung, was a college classmate of mine. He considered his main, if not the only, mission in Washington was to serve as the faithful proselytizer for Kim Dae-jung's "Sunshine Policy." Inasmuch as the newly elected U.S. President George W. Bush was not a great fan of the Policy, the situation did not bode well for a smooth relationship between the governments of Kim Dae-jung and George W. Bush, and later Roh Moo-hyun and George W. Bush.

But there was an even more urgent reason why Roh wanted me to go to Washington to represent him. Roh was elected on a platform that was, to say the least, quite critical of the U.S.' hard-line policy toward North Korea and South Korea's less than assertive posture toward the United States. Roh was known for uttering that famous declaration, "What's wrong with being anti-American?" When Roh asked me to go to Washington, he told me that he knew I did not vote for him, which was the reason why he wanted me to be his ambassador there. He wanted to get along well with the United States and wanted to send the U.S. the signal that he wanted to be America's friend. Roh was looking forward to his scheduled visit to Washington in May, where he wanted to establish a good personal rapport with President Bush. He thought I was the right choice to take up the task.

Lurking behind both of these two assignments, ten years apart, was the North Korean nuclear issue. Although I only had a vague sense about it at the time of my first government assignment, dealing with the threat of North Korean nuclear weapons and their development turned out to be my major and primary concern. Nuclear weapons themselves were not only a danger in their own right, but in the course of dealing with the issue, a devastating armed conflict and war was also a constant, looming possibility.

As a young boy of nine, I experienced the devastation of war and grew to know how important peace and security were for the country and people. I felt a heavy responsibility on my shoulders to resolve the issue peacefully and diplomatically in any way possible. This is an honest record of how I grew up to be interested in diplomacy, how I dealt with it when the opportunity and challenge came, what I feel I have been able to accomplish, and those things that I have failed to achieve.

Chapter I

Growing up

Born to a Family Rooted in Seoul for More Than Five Centuries

I was born in 1940, the 30th year of Japanese colonial rule, and five years before the end of the Second World War. In the summer of 1945, when I was a five-year-old boy, our family lived in a Korean-style house near Saemunan Church in Kwanghwamun, the center of the city of Seoul. I mention this house because it survived through the destruction of the Korean War and the city's reconstruction over the last half a century, until 2013. I presume that the old house was not touched because it was located on the church's property and was awaiting the renovation of the whole compound. I was always thrilled and proud to show my foreign friends who visited Seoul over the years that the house my family used to live in until the mid-1940s was still standing despite the plethora of new roads and high buildings around it.

It was such a disappointment when, one day, I took my foreign friends to that neighborhood to show them my childhood home, only to find that it had been razed to the ground to make room for a new building for the church. On that sunny day, I also remembered that

Han Hoon, five-year-old, 1945. (Hoon was my childhood name.)

back in the summer of 1945, we saw two shiny airplanes flying high and silently over our heads. Adults had told me that they were B-29 bombers. I did not know it then, but I later found out that those were the same planes that dropped the atomic bombs on Hiroshima and Nagasaki later that summer.

I was born to a family who had lived in Seoul for at least five centuries. According to the family register (known as *jokbo* in Korean), one of my great-grandfathers of 21 generations ago (1403-1456 AD) served as a deputy prime minister during the early part of the Joseon Dynasty and conducted diplomacy vis-à-vis China. My forefathers supposedly served as civil servants in the earlier period, but they were "demoted" to the military ranks, presumably because one of them was punished by the court for insubordination. I mention this part of my family history as a way of wondering if I inherited some DNA related to diplomacy from my ancestors.

As I was growing up, my great-grandfather, who had served as the court doctor for King Kojong at the end of the 19th century, recounted to me stories of his life and work in the court. He told me that in 1895, when Queen Myeongseong was assassinated by some Japanese intruders, he had given some tranquilizing medicine to the king who was in shock over the event. The king, after drinking the medicine, in his haste, wiped off his mouth with a towel that had been reserved to dry my great-grandfather's private parts. I could imagine the embarrassment he must have felt, even though he concealed this fact from the king.

My father was a self-made man who ran a school that taught driving and automobile repair. He also ran a company that operated buses and taxis. As such, we did not feel too strapped economically. But it was also a time when there was no regular market for automobile parts and fuel. As I witnessed how difficult it was for my father to run a business, I resolved to become a public servant rather than be involved in business or commerce. My mother did not have much formal education but taught herself to become a learned and intelligent lady. I remember her as being benevolent and wise, and she was the best role model I could ask for.

During the ten-year period between 1950 and 1960, three things happened that would affect the course of my life. The first was the Korean War that broke out in 1950, when I was a nine-year-old boy. The second was the opportunity I was given in 1956, when I was a tenth grader in high school, to travel to the United States to attend Camp Rising Sun, an international camp located in Rhinebeck, New York. The third was participating in a student uprising in 1960 known as the April Revolution during my junior year in college.

The Korean War (1950-1953) cost more than two million lives (mostly Koreans) and caused tremendous havoc for those who survived. The tragedy did not allow this nine-year-old boy to avoid it untouched. With my parents, I had to walk for several days to flee from bullets and bombs. We suffered from hunger and exhaustion. I witnessed battles being fought, saw prisoners of war being dragged away, and was hit by artillery shrapnel. Almost seventy years later, this shrapnel is still embedded in my hip.

The Korean War began on Sunday, June 25th, 1950. I was a fourth grader at Muhak Elementary School in the southeastern part of Seoul. As I remember, the summer recess was about to begin, and we were looking forward to several weeks when we could play around without going to school. On the day that the North Korean army crossed the 38th Parallel, which divided North and South Korea, we heard artillery in the distance and a bomb exploding from a small airplane.

Seoul was overrun by the North Korean "People's Army" on June 28th, only three days after they crossed over the 38th parallel which served as the demarcation line. On the evening of June 27th, my parents and I joined the evacuation group, walking over to Hangang Naru (Han River Ferry Point), about four kilometers from Wangshimni, where we lived, and were ferried across the river. We headed south on foot across the wet muddy field (today the upscale Apgujeong-dong district) to Maljuk-Kori.[1] It took us a couple of days of walking and hitching rides to reach a small town in South Chungcheong Province called Ryugu (about 120 kilometers from Seoul), where a friend of my father's lived. But within a few days, that area was overtaken by the advancing North Korean army, and so we returned to Seoul.

This time we traveled entirely on foot, and on the way we saw North Korean soldiers on the road stare piercingly at our family, led by my bourgeois-looking father. After a few days of walking, hungry and exhausted, we came back to Seoul and reached my grandfather's house in Changshin-dong, just outside the East Gate (Dongdaemun). There, for almost two and a half months during the North Korean occupation of Seoul, my father hid in the attic while the rest of our family went out to find food and other necessities.

---

1   In Korean, *maljuk* means boiled horse feed. We thought at the time that the place was called as such because the ground was wet and muddy. As we learned later, it used to be an area where a stagecoach station was located and horses were fed with boiled feed.

Between Life and Death

On September 15th, U.S. forces, which were sent to Korea by President Harry S. Truman[2] to stop the advancing North Koreans, made a surprise landing in Incheon under the command of General Douglas MacArthur. Together with South Korean marines who joined them, the U.S. forces advanced to Seoul to retake it from the North Koreans. On the evening of September 26th (1950), artillery shells and incendiary bombs rained down on some parts of Seoul, including the Changshin-dong area, where our family was staying. In the bombardment, I lost one of my aunts and my great-grandfather.

I was hit in the lower back by shrapnel from an exploding artillery shell. As I was bleeding profusely, my father took me on his back and we headed with my mother toward Uijeongbu, north of Seoul, where one of his friends lived. On the road, we encountered some of the retreating North Korean soldiers. One of them, when he saw me bleeding, took out a long cloth, which he said his mother had given him, and tied up my wound. I might have died if not for this soldier, to whom I still feel thankful. Forty years later, when I was serving as the South Korean Foreign Minister, this story appeared in a *New York Times* article written by David Sanger (December 28, 1993).[3] I was criticized by some conservative politicians at the time for having divulged this story of a good deed by a North Korean soldier.

---

2 President Truman's full name is sometimes written as Harry S Truman or more often as Harry S. Truman. In fact, he signed his name as Harry S. Truman (with a period) in some official documents. He authored a biography under the name Harry S. Truman. When he was born in 1884, his parents couldn't decide on a middle name and simply went with the letter S, to honor his paternal grandfather (Shippe) and his maternal grandfather (Solomon). In this book, we will use the name Harry S. Truman (with a period) as that is the way he signed his name in official documents.

3 http://www.nytimes.com/1993/12/28/world/seoul-journal-a-korean-voice-forceful-but-almost-inaudible.html

During the war, I was not only struck by the shrapnel of an artillery shell, but I also narrowly missed being hit by rocket fire from a fighter plane. I also witnessed American prisoners of war being herded by North Korean soldiers and a firefight between North and South Korean troops.

In December 1950, the South Korean and U.S. forces, which had advanced close to the Chinese border, had to retreat again after the Chinese People's Liberation Army (PLA) intervened in the Korean War. During what was known as "January 4th Retreat" (1951) from Seoul, our extended family, including in-laws from my mother's side, used a truck to go all the way to Busan. It was a vehicle that the North Korean army had brought with them during the invasion and left in Seoul during their retreat. Somehow, my father had gotten hold of it after the September recapture of the city.

In Busan, we found housing in Oncheon-dong, Dongrae, in the outskirts of the city. I attended the Naeseong Elementary School in Dongrae for a few months before transferring to a makeshift school for those who had fled from Seoul. Those I had met at Naeseong Elementary kindly considered me as their classmate, and I continued to meet a few of them until recently. In the makeshift school, classes were conducted outdoors, not having any buildings, roofs, desks, or chairs. In 2014, a Korean movie was released with the title "Ode to My Father." It depicted the turbulent life story of a family who were among the thousands of refugees transported south by the U.S. Navy ship, the USS Meredith Victory, in what was known as the Hungnam Evacuation of 1950. I mention this movie because the school that Yun Deok-Su, the hero of the movie, attended as a nine-year-old boy, the same age as me at the time, was very similar to my outdoor school. But the school in the movie was better equipped than mine—it had desks and chairs.

It was probably a combination of good luck and a decent score on the qualifying examination that, in 1952, I was admitted to Kyunggi

Middle School, a rather competitive school which was taking refuge in Busan during the war. Its makeshift buildings were located in the Kudeok-san area in southwestern Busan. It was a long distance from where we lived, and I had to struggle to find transportation. Every day I took a combination of trolley, bus, and even the back of a truck to go to and from school.

The next year, in the spring of 1953, the war had not formally ended, but our family decided to return to Seoul, as many of the "refugee" middle schools were moving back.[4] But returning to Seoul was as hard as fleeing from it. There was a temporary railroad bridge crossing the Han River, and securing passes was difficult and the checks on the train were very severe and slow.

Arriving in Seoul, we found the city in near total ruins. There were hardly any remaining buildings because of the aerial and artillery bombings. There was no public transportation. As a result of the war, which produced more than two million casualties in three years, Seoul had become a city of ruins and waste, a city that needed to be rebuilt from scratch.

An 8th Grader Cries: "No Truce! March North!"

Several months after our return to Seoul, I became embroiled in demonstrations opposing the ceasefire and truce in Korea. Merely in our second year of middle school, my schoolmates were riled up by upper classmen and ran out into the streets to shout, "March north and achieve unification!" Citizens cheered us on and brought buckets of water to help us quench our thirst on the hot summer days.

---

4   At the time, middle schools were comprised of grades 7-12, before the division between middle and high schools.

With my father, on a sojourn to Dokjok-do, 1956

The United States, which had already witnessed some 30,000 killed in the Korean War, elected General Dwight D. Eisenhower as president in 1952. A hero in the European theatre of World War II, he had made ending the Korean War a major campaign promise. After assuming office, President Eisenhower pursued negotiations with North Korea for an armistice. But in South Korea, the Syngman Rhee government, which made "anti-communism and unification" a national slogan, was steadfastly opposing any truce until unification could be achieved. As college students had not yet begun to participate in political activities in earnest, it was the middle and high school students who took the lead in a movement to oppose the truce without unification. Eventually, the United States was able to coax the Rhee government to accept the armistice with the promise of a Korea-U.S. Mutual Defense Treaty and massive economic aid for Korea's post-war reconstruction.

People in South Korea accepted the armistice with a mixed feeling of regret for not achieving unification but also of relief for ending the destructive war. I was still at a tender age, but my experience in the war taught me how devastating, cruel, and fearful war could be and that it had to be avoided at all cost. Nevertheless, it was only after I graduated from college and entered adulthood that I had some understanding of the causes and meaning of the Korean War.

With my mother, 1953

Who Invaded Whom

The war ended with an armistice signed on July 27, 1953. But for some time, controversy remained regarding the cause and precipitator of the war. There were three theories about the origin of the Korean War. Most people in South Korea and the United States believed that North Korean President Kim Il-sung planned and carried out the invasion of the South. A second group of people, much smaller in number, argued that the United States was responsible for the war because it left Korea divided into North and South, propped up the South Korean government, and even induced, if inadvertently, North Korea to invade the South with such pronouncements as the Acheson Declaration of January 1950, which excluded Korea from the U.S. "defensive perimeter."[5]

Finally, a small minority of ideologues believed that the initial provocation which led to the Korean War was by the South Koreans. According to this theory, South Korea attacked the North first, and North Korea merely counter-attacked in response. Not many people subscribe to this theory now, but after the fighting stopped in Korea, the theory wielded some influence in the intellectual circles in the United States.[6] But it is far from the truth to say that the South could have either attacked the North in a major way or purposefully induced the North to attack the South. How can one explain the fact that Seoul was overrun by the North Korean army only three days after the war broke out?

Of these "theories," the one that we can consider as the soundest argument is the first one, that North Korea invaded the South, period. The North Korean regime of Kim Il-sung planned the invasion and launched a large-scale surprise attack. Supported by the Soviet Union, which was pursuing an expansionist policy, North Korea attempted to conquer the South militarily. According to this analysis, if it had not been for the intervention of the United States and the United Nations, South Korea would have been easily taken over by the North. In fact, secret Soviet documents on the Korean War released by post-Soviet Russia in the 1990s confirmed that this analysis is based on facts.

---

5   In a similar vein, the scholar Bruce Cumings wrote in his book, *The Origins of the Korean War* (1988), "[Wars] originate in multiple causes, with blame enough to go around for everyone—and blame enough to include Americans who thoughtlessly divided Korea and then reestablished the colonial government machinery and the Koreans who served it."

6   I. F. Stone, an American radical journalist and writer, argued that South Korea, with the connivance and support of the United States, provoked North Korea to attack the South (*The Hidden History of the Korean War, 1950-51* [1952]).

Discovering the English Language

In order to explain the second major event during my early years, attending an international camp in the United States, it is necessary to explain how I became interested in learning English. After I entered middle school (7th to 9th grade), where they taught elementary English, I became interested in learning the language and found it easy and fun to learn.

A few methods helped me to become familiar with the English language. First was to study hard what we were being taught in school, such as grammar and composition. The second was to find an instructor who was a native speaker of English. At the time, we could not find a professional English teacher, so a couple of friends and I went to the front gate of the U.S. Signal Corps compound which was located near the East Gate in Seoul and struck up conversation (in very halting English) with young G.I.s passing by. We asked them if any one of them would be interested in teaching us conversational English.

It was our good luck that one of them, a soldier named Richard F. Call, who (we learned later) attended a teachers' college in Maine, willingly agreed to teach us English. Subsequently, we had afterschool classes for a couple of hours every weekday for nearly two years. Richard turned out to be a dedicated teacher. With virtually no compensation, he enthusiastically taught us not only English, but also about American culture and way of life. Even today, some people say that I have a tinge of New England accent in my English, which I attribute to my learning the language from Richard Call, who was from the region.

The third method was to listen to AFKN (American Forces Korea Network), a radio broadcasting for the U.S. forces stationed in Korea, but which was also available to Korean listeners. I can still

With English teacher Mr. Call, in the back row. I am in front of him, in checkered shirt, 1953.

remember some of the announcements in its programs, such as "At the beginning of another day, we present to you a silent moment of religious meditation..." The announcer had such a solemn voice and clear pronunciation that I cannot forget it, even today.

I sometimes watched American movies with Korean subtitles. At the time, middle school students were not allowed to go to the movies individually, so I had to violate the rules in order to see the movies that I wanted. If possible, I enjoyed seeing the same movie several times so that I could memorize the dialogue. I was thrilled by the movie "National Velvet," starring Mickey Rooney and a young Elizabeth Taylor, and I was heart-broken by "Waterloo Bridge" with Vivian Leigh and Robert Taylor.

The fourth way to improve my English ability was to join the Student Cultural Club (SCC), an English-speaking society organized by some students older than me. Members of SCC met on a weekly basis at a space provided by the United States Information Service

Poster for movie, "National Velvet"

With Student Cultural Club members, 1959
I am second from right.

(USIS), which was then under the direction of the U.S. embassy's cultural attaché. We had discussion meetings, sang English songs, and conversed in English, even if not fluently. We sometimes invited guests from the U.S. embassy and visited the U.S. military base in Yongsan. For me, it was an English "immersion" experience.

With Yi Song-mi, 1962

Many of the SCC members later became prominent members of Korean society, and as of 2018 we have quarterly gatherings. In addition to learning English, being a member of the SCC gave me another gift of my life, which was to meet a young woman named Yi Song-mi, who was then a student at the College of Fine Arts at Seoul National University. We got married and have been life partners for over half a century.

Meeting a New World

During my first year of high school (10th grade), I received a special opportunity to visit the United States. It was "special" because, at that time, even ordinary citizens in Korea, much less a young high school boy, would have rarely had an opportunity to travel abroad. I was selected to participate in an international summer scholarship camp called Camp Rising Sun (CRS), located in a town called Rhinebeck, New York, in the Catskills. The camp was established in 1927 by the philanthropist George E. Jonas for the purpose of bringing together young campers (14-15 years of age) from around the world for friendship, cultural understanding, and leadership training. When I attended the camp, there were about 50 campers, about half of them coming from the United States and the rest from some twenty other countries, including Central America (Mexico), Asia (Korea, Japan,

With my father at Yeouido Airport, 1956

With "boys from abroad" at Camp Rising Sun, 1956

Pakistan, Indonesia, India, etc.), and Europe (England, France, Germany, Sweden, Denmark, and Finland).

The task of selecting and sending off the campers to the United States from some Asian countries was administered by the Asia Foundation, which had been established in 1954 and opened an office in Seoul the following year. The Asia Foundation was founded and funded by the U.S. government as a non-governmental organization devoted to promoting relations between Asia and America, and development of Asia (including democracy, rule of law, and economic and social development).

In the spring of 1956, the Asia Foundation's Seoul office (headed by Mary C. Walker) sent out a notice to a few high schools in Seoul soliciting recommendations for candidates to attend Camp Rising Sun. I was recommended by Kyonggi High School, and was subsequently selected after an interview with the panel at a meeting room in the foundation office in Kwanhoon-dong, downtown Seoul.

Thus, I was given the unexpected opportunity to attend the camp. In the course of this experience I was able to gain some understanding of the United States as a country and learn more about its customs and language. It also gave me the opportunity to meet boys from over 20 countries with whom I lived, played, and tented together for two months. I am certain that this exposure to the outside world during my youth became a strong reason for my interest and motivation to pursue a career in diplomacy.

Reflecting the ideals of the camp, aimed at promoting peace and providing leadership training, it was run in a frugal and wholesome way. Campers lived in tents, did their own laundry, did the kitchen work (including washing dishes and peeling potatoes), cleaned the grounds, and of course made their own beds. Not having had any camp experience growing up in Korea, at the time, everything was new and challenging to me.

CRS was (and still is) a "scholarship camp," where the basic housing and living expenses are covered by the camp. My traveling expenses, including airfare and insurance, were paid for by the Asia Foundation. I remember the round trip airfare was about $1,100. Considering that the per capita GDP of Korea at the time was only $66, it was indeed quite a large amount.

The Asia Foundation is still active in several Asian countries. But in the past several decades, Korea has transformed itself from a recipient of foreign aid to a provider. Today, I am serving as the Chairman of the Friends of the Asia Foundation (FOTAF) which raises funds to support projects in Asia on behalf of the Asia Foundation. As for Camp Rising Sun, Korea still sends campers every summer and there is now not only a CRS for boys, but also one for girls (since 1990).

My trip to the United States took place only three years after the end of the Korean War and Korea was still in the process of recovery and reconstruction. As high school students had to have their heads shaved like Buddhist monks, I had to get the permission to grow my hair an inch or so before departing Seoul. I arrived in the United States in my summer uniform, which was a short sleeve shirt with my name tag on it. I was wearing what was known as "walker shoes," which were

My first visit to New York, 1956

actually high necked army boots which were most popular among the Korean youths then. I am sure I must have looked rather strange to the American hosts who met me, but nobody seemed to mind my outfit.

The route to the camp was long and tiring. There was no direct flight from Seoul to New York, and I had layovers in Tokyo (one day), Wake Island for a fuel stop (I flew Pan American for the cross-Pacific flight), overnight in Honolulu (before Hawaii acquired its statehood), and San Francisco, where I stayed for two days with a host family in beautiful Berkeley Hills. Six days later, I finally arrived in New York at Idlewild airport (which was the name of the airport before it was changed to JFK).

Before attending CRS, my image of the United States was formed through movies and an English language textbook called Dixon, which described and had drawings of suburban American life. I enjoyed the cartoon, "Blondie," as well. I expected to have a comfortable life with some luxury in America. But I had to leave the care of my parents for the first time in my life to attend the camp, and I had to do household chores, got a lot of mosquito bites (American mosquitoes being much bigger and fiercer than Korean ones), and had occasional home-sickness.

In the process, however, I learned a great deal about America, other countries and peoples, and the excitement and breadth of the outside world. I matured considerably. Even though the camp was located in the eastern part of the United States, I could feel the pioneer spirit of the Americans I met. They also impressed me as being frugal, diligent, and for the most part, generous.

Because visiting the United States was such a rare thing, especially for a high school boy, I was known and usually introduced as "the one who visited America" after I returned home. As I was told by my mother to be humble and not to be boastful, I think I became even more reticent to talk about myself or show off after my visit to the United States. I think that it was not a coincidence that I went on to get my Master's degree at the University of New Hampshire and that my first teaching job was at Brooklyn College in New York. Both, at least in part, were attributable to the fact that I experienced CRS in upstate New York when a boy.

Another Moment of Life and Death

My father suddenly passed away in an accident in 1957. Even during the mourning period of about a year, I studied for the college entrance examination, and was admitted to Seoul National University (SNU) as a political science major.

Why did I choose to study politics? The year 1958, when I entered college, was the peak of President Syngman Rhee's dictatorship.

With high-school mates, I am last on the right. 1958

Corruption was rampant, politics was disorderly, and there was much social disruption. Everytime an election was held, there was controversy about whether it was fair and clean. In fact, elections used to be full of fraud and violence. Voting secrecy was violated, opposition candidates were harassed, and there was even *en masse* vote tampering.

I wanted to better understand the dynamics of politics and society and contribute to the further development of the country. That's why I applied for the politics department. Two years later, the department split into two departments: political science and diplomacy. By that time, I had become more interested in international relations, which is one reason why I became a student in the department of diplomacy. Other reasons were that I was becoming more confident with the English language and more interested in a diplomatic career.

Then the April 19th student uprising of 1960 erupted in protest over the fraudulent election held the previous month, as well as President Syngman Rhee's dictatorship and failures in governance. Students first took to the streets to demand the return of democracy and removal of what was then called the "wall of cronies" around the president. I later joined them with a group of students from my own university.

There were other incidents that served as the fuses for the April 19th uprising. On April 11th, in Masan, a high school student was found dead with a teargas canister lodged in his head. On April 18th, dozens of protesting Korea University students were violently attacked by hooligans in Seoul's downtown area, Jongro. Although the April 19th demonstration was being planned in advance before these events took place, they no doubt contributed to intensifying the protests.

At the time, there was no noticeable student political movements in the university campuses, as there came to be a few years later. I, for one, was not a political activist. The reason why students such as me, who used to quietly concentrate on school work, decided to actively join the protests was that they all felt that it was necessary to do something about the situation, which was terribly wrong and unjust.

On April 19th, I set out for school in my usual black-dyed army fatigues, which served as the school uniform for many students at that time. At ten o'clock, we went into the library to announce to the students that we were going to march and demonstrate against the election fraud and the Syngman Rhee dictatorship and to ask them to join the demonstration.

We poured out of the front gate of the SNU Dongsung-dong campus and marched to the National Assembly building, which was near Kwanghwamun at the time. After a rally and several speeches, a few of us marched over to Hyoja-dong where the presidential compound called Kyungmu-dae (now the Blue House) was located. By the time we arrived there, the street leading to the president's compound was already filled with students from another school, Dongkuk University. There was also a barricade set up to block the further advance of the students toward the compound. The road was blocked by dozens of policemen lined up behind the barricade with rifles in their hands.

Female students demonstrating on April 19, 1960. Yi Song-mi,
my future wife, is seen in a circle.

As we reached about 50 meters from the barricade, the policemen started to fire live ammunition indiscriminately toward us. The demonstrators hit the ground at the sudden bursts of gunfire, and I recognized from my military training that they were live bullets that were flying above our heads. As I lay flat on the ground while the guns were being fired, I could see scenes of my young life as if in a kaleidoscope. After a while, I crawled to the side of the street and ran into the classroom of a girls' high school nearby. The students treated me like a hero. I learned later that, on that street at that time, some 50 demonstrators lost their lives and dozens were wounded. Having survived an artillery shrapnel wound during the Korean War and gun bullets raining down during the student protest ten years later, I feel that I was very lucky indeed.

As a result of the April 19th student uprising, the dictatorship was driven out and democracy seemed to have been installed. What is known in Korea as "4-19" showed that unrighteous authority cannot stay in power eternally. Unfortunately, however, the "people's will" lacked the leadership which could translate democracy into an institutional reality.

With college friends, 1960. I am the first on the left in the front row.

The opposition Democratic Party was split into two factions, "old" and "new," and the government that was subsequently formed could neither create nor defend a new order. As a result, it gave way to a military coup d'état within a year of its formation, resulting in another dictatorship.

After graduating from college, I had the opportunity to work at the international broadcasting station of KBS, the Korean Broadcasting System. I had a job in the "Voice of Free Korea" section, a radio program broadcast in foreign languages, mainly English. I gathered news, served as a script-writer and broadcaster, and did news analysis. It was a hard but fulfilling experience that proved to be helpful for my work later as a graduate student in the United States. The experience taught me how to search for data, analyze it, and write a coherent report within a given deadline. The experience also helped my being selected as a recipient of the Fulbright scholarship when I went to the United States for graduate school.

Chapter 2

Preparing a Career

Graduate Student Days in the U.S.

The Fulbright scholarship I received in 1962 paid for a large portion of the expenses required for my study in the United States, including travel and insurance. It was both an honor to receive the scholarship and a substantial source of monetary support, as annually there were only one or two recipients from Korea selected for the Fulbright. It also helped to secure admission to a U.S. university.

I chose the University of New Hampshire (UNH) in Durham, N.H. as my first school because it was a decent state university, and I thought both the location and size were convenient and manageable for my study and life in America. As I started my study at UNH, I found out that, in order to major in political science in America, I should be well versed in U.S. politics. But that was an area that I was quite weak in, as I did not have the opportunity to focus on the topic before going to America.

It was also a time when the study of political behavior ("behaviorism" as they called it) was becoming fashionable, and that approach focused on American politics. Thus, much of my time during my first year in the United States was taken up by studying the American political system. It turned out to be useful later on. Actually, when I went on to do my Ph.D. at the University of California, Berkeley two years later, I often served as a teaching assistant in American politics.

In this remote and lonely place in Durham, New Hampshire, my morale and intellectual support was boosted by an older Camp Rising Sun alumnus, Maurice Richter, who was teaching as a professor in the sociology department at UNH. Professor Richter helped me to understand and adjust to America and its university life.

After a year of study at UNH, I was appointed as a teaching assistant to teach international politics. I was not sure if I was good enough for the appointment, but it certainly was both a challenge and honor for me. The topic of my M.A. thesis was "The Politics of Foreign Policy of the Syngman Rhee Government." Although the thesis was supposed to focus on South Korea's foreign relations, particularly U.S.-Korea relations, much of it spilt over into Korean domestic politics.

The University of California, Berkeley, where I chose to do my

With Professor John T. Holden, 1993

Ph.D., was often cited as one of the top-ranked universities, especially at the graduate level. It was a perfect school for me, as it had many distinguished professors in the field of political science, and I was offered a good scholarship. Also, the school is located in an area with very moderate weather and beautiful surroundings. After studying at UNH, a modest sized university, I thought I would take up the challenges of a bigger university and experience the American university in full.

On an August day in 1964, my wife Song-mi and I set out from Durham, New Hampshire, to drive to California in a 1956 Chevrolet. We took out the back seat of the car and put in its place a crib for our five-month old baby boy, Charles. The cross country trip, mainly on interstate highway route #95, took us one week.

As we were preparing to leave, the elderly chairman of the department, Professor John T. Holden, came to our rented house and knocked at the door. He had a smile across his face as he told us that he had just received one thousand dollars from an anonymous donor, who asked him to convey it to us for our journey across the country. He would not tell me who gave the money. I still remember his parting words: "Now you can have some steaks on your way to California." One thousand dollars was quite a large amount, as my salary as a teaching assistant then was only about $200 per month. I could only guess who the anonymous donor was. It must have been Mr. George Jonas (we called him "Freddie"), the founder of CRS.

Witnessing a Student Movement in the U.S.

I found the Berkeley campus very political, in contrast to the almost apolitical atmosphere at the University of New Hampshire. In 1964, when we arrived at Berkeley, a student movement called "The Free

Free Speech movement at Berkeley in 1960s.

Speech Movement" was very active under the leadership of a sociology student from New York, Mario Savio. Every day at noon, there was a rally at the Sproul Plaza in front of the administration building to the left of the Sather Gate which was designated as one of the California Historical Landmarks. The students were demanding free speech and an end to the Vietnam War.

Subsequently, the student protest evolved into a full scale movement against the government and the war not only in Vietnam, but also in Cambodia, which the United States bombed and invaded in the course of waging the war.

As the demonstration became more intense and violent, California's governor Ronald Reagan even ordered National Guard helicopters to spray tear gas on the students from the air.

The anti-war student movement that started in Berkeley spread to throughout the United States. At Kent State University in Ohio, members of the Ohio National Guard shot at unarmed demonstrators, killing four students and wounding nine others. After this tragic event, all over the

United States, millions of college students went on strike. At universities such as Columbia and Cornell, violent demonstrations took place. As one who took part in the April 19th student uprising in Korea and was shot at during the demonstration, I had an acute feeling of empathy toward the protesting students.

Professor Scalapino

I learned and experienced a great deal while studying at Berkeley for six years. One teacher I met there was Professor Robert A. Scalapino (1919-2011), a well-known specialist on East Asian politics. As his research assistant, I helped him with his book-writing, and we traveled together. In 1968, when Professor and Mrs. Scalapino (Dee) visited Korea, I toured the country with them, from Seoul to Busan and Kwangju, and back to Seoul.

After I finished my doctorate, I had the chance to meet Professor

With Professor Scalapino at his 90th Birthday.

Scalapino in many international conferences and seminars. He was well-known among specialists, not only for his prolific and excellent writings, but also for his ability to draw summaries and conclusions from conferences. He was not only a superb scholar but also a warm-hearted and broad-minded person. Professor Scalapino was a rock of support for me when I was his student and afterwards.

One example of this is how I was able to quit smoking, a habit I acquired while serving in the Korean army. One day, without much thinking, I was smoking in the living room of the professor's home in the Berkeley Hills overlooking the beautiful San Francisco Bay. He did not say anything then, but later, he quietly asked me: "You look like a smart young man, but why do you still smoke?" Those words turned out to be a great gift for me, as I decided to quit the bad habit there and then.

In the summer of 1975, I was recommended by my department to serve as an intern at the United Nations Development Programme (UNDP), which was established to provide technical assistance for socio-economic development in such fields as health, environment, and energy. As an intern, I was given the task of administering a support program for the utilization of thermal energy and hot spring water in Turkey. Although Korea was not yet a member of the United Nations, I had the opportunity to work for the first time in an international organization and interact with staff members from various countries. The experience also gave me some understanding of how an international organization operated. I even considered working there after this short stint (of two months) was over. However, I decided to continue towards my original goal of pursuing an academic career.

At Berkeley, it took me six years to finish my doctorate in political science. At that point, I was unsure if I would return to Korea with the degree or seek a professorship in the United States, even for a short time. Eventually, I chose the latter and took a job as assistant professor

Receiving Peter Odegard Award, 1969

at Brooklyn College of the City University of New York, which had both excellent students and a strong faculty.

While I was enjoying teaching at Brooklyn College, my wife Song-mi, an art historian with a master's degree from Berkeley, was working as a part-time instructor for community colleges in New York. In 1975, she applied for admission to a Ph.D. program in Art History at Princeton University in New Jersey and was admitted. We decided it was best that the whole family to move to Princeton where the university was located, even though that meant I would have to commute from Princeton to Brooklyn (a two and a half hour-drive) two or three times a week.

On days that I did not have to commute, I was able to take advantage of the first-rate libraries in Princeton, such as the East Asian Library (Jones Library) and the central Firestone Library, which had a rich collection of books, materials, and research equipment. Taking advantage of Princeton's research facilities, I was able to write several articles published in major journals. At the same time, I was able to take Japanese language classes at the university to hone my Japanese skills.

Even though my commuting hours were long, it was a big boon for me to be able to use the scholarly infrastructure at Princeton University.

My seven years' teaching at an American university helped not only with my research, but also to gain a better understanding of the management functions and administrative inner workings of a college and the culture of academia in the United States. I also devoted some of my time to promote exchanges between scholars of Korea and the United States.

However, because the 1970s was a period of the authoritarian "Yushin" system in Korea, there was much friction between Korea and the United States. The U.S. government was critical of the Park Chung -hee regime of South Korea for its suppression of human rights and retreat from democracy. For that reason, some American academics even refused to engage in exchanges with their Korean counterparts.

During my tenure at Brooklyn College (which was within the City University of New York system), something very unfortunate took place for the city administration. The city went bankrupt as a result of over-spending. At the time, as an employee of the City University of New York and a resident of New Jersey, I was paying taxes to four entities— the federal government, New Jersey State, New York State and the City of New York. Because the City was bankrupt, my paycheck stopped coming. As a result, I faced the humiliating experience of standing in line for unemployment compensation at a federal office in New Jersey. The only silver-lining of this situation was that it helped me to gain a better understanding of how the federal and local governments operated. It also reinforced my decision to return home to Korea and do something more worthwhile with my life.

Return to Korea and Professorship at Korea University

Before the bankruptcy in New York City, I had been promoted to associate professor and granted lifetime tenure at Brooklyn College. But thankfully, shortly after the bankruptcy episode, I was offered a professorship at Korea University in Seoul. The person who approached me with the offer was none other than Professor Kim Jun-yop, who was concurrently serving as the director of the well known Asiatic Research Center (ARC) at the university. Professor Kim, for whom I had high respect, told me that I was to succeed Professor Kim Kyung-won, who took a job at the Blue House as an international relations advisor.

I was not a graduate of Korea University. However, I had quite a few personal ties with the school. My aunt's husband, the late Professor Kim Soon-shik, who was considered the leading scholar in accounting, served as the graduate school dean and dean of the school of business administration. My father-in-law, Professor Yi Hong-jik, who was a pillar in the field of Korean history, served as the museum director.

After arriving at the university, where I started to teach in the fall of 1978, I also became involved with the activities of the ARC. The organization was actively engaged in intellectual exchanges with institutes in other countries, such as the United States and Japan. At the time, the ARC stood out among university research institutes in fundraising, research, and international exchanges. Its main foreign research funds came from such sources as the Ford Foundation and Rockefeller Foundation in the United States and Konrad Adenauer Stiftung in West Germany.

The ARC's major activities were focused on the unification issue and Korea's relations with major countries like the United States, Japan, and China. Until the 1970s and even into the 1980s, research on subjects related to communist countries was very restricted in Korea.

Visit to the Middle East with Professor Kim Sang-hyop

The use of materials on communism and communist countries was virtually prohibited. There was even a case in which the sale of a book was interrupted simply because it contained the word "people" in the title ("people" as in People's Liberation Army). Conducting intellectual exchanges with Japanese institutes was also politically difficult, as there was a great deal of animosity and lingering grievances toward Japan over their thirty-five year rule of Korea from 1910 to 1945.

However, because of the reputation that Professor Kim Jun-yop had as a patriot and a man of impeccable integrity, the ARC had the permission to deal with so-called "unhealthy" (meaning related to communism) materials and publications and engage in intellectual exchange with Japan. As a member of the ARC, I was able to broaden my intellectual contacts with scholars and experts of other countries and gain a deeper understanding of Korea's relations with them.

One noteworthy project was with the Japan Center for International Exchange (JCIE), under the leadership of its chairman, Tadashi Yamamoto. Yamamoto, a leading internationalist and proponent of strengthening nongovernmental ties between Japan and other countries, was dedicated to the cause of improving relations between Korea and Japan. My association with Yamamoto lasted for nearly four decades until he passed away in 2012. We worked closely together within the context of semi-governmental committees focusing on Korea-Japan relations.

A few months after I started to teach at Korea University, the university's President, Kim Sang-hyop, asked me if I would join him on his inspection tour of the Middle East in Saudi Arabia and Kuwait. I was happy to accompany him, as it was an excellent opportunity to visit the region where, at the time, Korean construction companies were involved in several large projects.

I was impressed with the size of the Korean work force and the organized and disciplined way they operated. I had nothing but praise and admiration for the workers who toiled months and sometimes years away from their homes and families. The weather was tolerable when we visited the Middle East, as it was winter. However, when I was told that the temperature could reach 40 or 50 degrees Celsius in summer, my admiration for these hardworking Koreans went up that much more.

In 1979, the year after I returned to Korea, the strongman president, Park Chung-hee, was gunned down by his intelligence chief, and a military junta led by General Chun Doo-hwan took over. In September 1980, General Chun became the acting president, and in March the following year, was "elected," in what was known as the "stadium election." Chun was voted in by hand-picked delegates in a sports stadium to serve as the 12th President of the Republic of Korea.

Also in September 1980, President Chun appointed as his senior economic advisor Dr. Kim Jae-ik, my brother-in-law and high school and college senior by two years. Jae-ik was criticized by some of his friends who objected to his serving under what they considered the

With Kim Jae-ik and his son, 1982

military dictatorship. However, he stayed with his decision to work for Chun, arguing that his service was not for the president, but for the nation and the people. Before Kim was officially appointed as the advisor, he served as the president's tutor in economics.

After President Chun assumed office, he was getting tutored not only in economics, but on diplomacy, trade, and regional affairs. At the recommendation of Dr. Kim Kyong-won, my predecessor at Korea University who became the president's chief of staff, I was asked to give President Chun briefings on U.S. politics and Korea-U.S. relations. I gave three early morning two-hour sessions on the subject. Although Chun was known to have one-sided conversations with his interlocutors later on, during the early period of his presidency, he was acting like an earnest and diligent student when I was tutoring him on the subjects that interested him.

Enlarging the Scope of Activities

In 1982, Professor Kim Jun-yop, director of the ARC for two decades, became the president of Korea University and designated me as his successor. In addition to promoting research, key activities of the center involved conducting international academic and intellectual exchanges and establishing personal ties with scholars and experts in other countries. As the leader of this institute, I tried to strengthen ties with academic institutions and individuals abroad by participating in or organizing international meetings and projects. By doing so, I strived to contribute to Korea's overall diplomacy as well. One such effort was the project on intellectual exchange with Japan.

At the time, Korea-Japan relations were not as smooth and cordial as they were during much of the post-World War II period. Korea, a proud and independent country of several millennia until its colonization by Japan in 1910, was ruled by fiat and oppression for 35 years until 1945 when it was liberated after Japan's surrender to the United States at the end of World War II.

South Korea's first president, Dr. Syngman Rhee, had made the slogan "oppose communism and reject Japan" a national motto and policy. It was only after General Park

Professor Kim Jun-yop

Chung-hee assumed the presidency in 1963 that negotiations started between Korea and Japan to "normalize" relations. In 1965, they concluded an agreement by which Japan would make an $800 million compensation payment to Korea, and their diplomatic relations would be restored. Nevertheless, their relations remained troubled and often hostile for another two decades, until the 1980s.

Under the circumstances, any intellectual exchange project with Japan was bound to be controversial in Korea. However, because of Professor Kim Jun-yop's credentials as a former anti-Japanese fighter, it was possible to conduct a Japan-related project without inviting criticism and controversy at the ARC.

The ARC-JCIE intellectual exchange project tackled not only issues related to economic cooperation, trade, and youth exchanges, but also thorny political issues such as territorial claims, history, and textbooks. As a result of these efforts, in August of 1988, the two governments of Korea and Japan agreed to launch a joint committee to discuss modern relations between the two countries for the 21st century. Professor Koh Byong-ik, a respected professor of history at Seoul National University, assumed the position of the Korean co-chair of the Committee, and I was to serve as a member and coordinator.

In that capacity, I tried to contribute to the development of Korean-Japanese relations that were constructive and future-oriented. In the report that the Committee submitted to both governments in 1990, we proposed *inter alia* the following: 1) to cast off the disagreements of the past and chart a constructive future; 2) to hold government consultations on school textbooks in each country; 3) to strengthen and expand economic cooperation; 4) to establish a cultural exchange fund; and 5) to strengthen and expand youth exchange programs between Korea and Japan. In recognition of my contribution to Korea-Japan relations with this committee and afterwards, the emperor of Japan bestowed on me

Visit to PM Yasuhiro Nakasone with former Korean PM Nam Duk-woo, 1987

the Grand Cordon of the Rising Sun in 2016.

In addition to my work at the ARC, I was involved in two activities that became the precursors of the Asia-Pacific Economic Cooperation (APEC) established in 1989 as a response to the growing interdependence of the Asia-Pacific.

One was the Williamsburg Conference, launched by the Asia Society in 1973 with the purpose of bringing together leaders from Asia, North America, and Oceania in government, academia, economy, business, culture, and journalism to discuss policy issues and foster friendship and understanding among the participants. I became a regular participant in this conference, which was held on an annual basis. I had the opportunity not only to learn about the issues, but also to form friendships with leaders in various fields from these countries. When I became South Korea's minister of foreign affairs in 1993 and attended governmental meetings such as ASEAN+3, APEC, and ARF (Asean Regional Forum), many of the participants of those meetings were familiar faces. It was as if they were gatherings of Williamsburg old boys.

The second was the Pacific Economic Cooperation Conference (PECC), which had its first meeting in Australia's capital, Canberra, in 1979. The rationale for launching PECC was that the center of the world economy was moving from the Atlantic to the Pacific, and that the countries in the region should strengthen and expand their cooperation and exchanges. The PECC meeting started with the participation of three members each from the government, academia, and economic/business sectors of the United States, Southeast Asian countries, Japan, Korea, Australia, New Zealand, and Canada.

The agenda of the first meeting included economic cooperation and integration among participating countries. The PECC eventually led to the creation of APEC, which was an inter-governmental organization that functioned as a non-governmental organization. Having a strong interest in cooperation and integration among the countries of the Asia-Pacific region, I was actively involved in both the Williamsburg meetings and PECC deliberations.

I Became a *Newsweek* Columnist

In the course of engaging in international activities, I had the opportunity to meet many foreign journalists and developed friendships with several of them. At the time, the director of the international information office of the Korean government, Park Shin-il, was my high school mate, and he would usually make arrangements for foreign journalists who visited Korea to interview me about Korea's internal politics and foreign relations. For that reason, I had the opportunity to talk and think about Korea's key issues. I learned much from the information and knowledge the journalists shared with me, and, simultaneously, I was able to organize my thoughts about issues thanks to the meaningful questions they asked.

One day in 1984, Tracy Dahlby, who was then Tokyo bureau chief of *Newsweek*, asked me if I would be interested in writing columns for the magazine. Until then, I occasionally wrote columns for newspapers like the *New York Times*, *Asian Wall Street Journal*, and *International Herald Tribune*, but I had not written columns for any newspaper or magazine on

Newsweek August 31, 1992

a regular basis. I gladly took up the challenge and, as a test case, wrote the first piece for the April 30, 1984 issue of *Newsweek* under the title, "Tokyo Tackles the Korea Issue." With that, I joined the distinguished list of *Newsweek* columnists, including Theo Sommer of Germany (*Die Zeit*) and George Will of the United States (*Washington Post*).

When I was later appointed as the minister of foreign affairs in the spring of 1993, I received a letter from the *Newsweek* headquarters in New York, thanking me for having written columns over the past ten years and informing me that I could be relieved from the task, now that I was South Korea's foreign minister. This suited me fine, as I would have neither the time nor the intent to continue as a columnist.

My last column appeared on December 21, 1992, with the title, "The Benefits of Apathy." The article pointed out that the 1992 presidential election, which was a competition among three candidates (Kim Young-sam, Kim Dae-jung, and Chung Ju-young), did not elicit the kind of fever and interest as in the past, as the election did not pit democracy against autocracy. The election could be seen, I argued, as a reflection of the fact that Korean democracy was maturing.

In any case, my ten-year "romance" with *Newsweek* came to a close when I became South Korea's foreign minister. During the period in which I wrote the columns, I had to pay close attention to South Korea's domestic politics. Because it was during the "Fifth Republic" period of President Chun Doo-hwan, who was considered as a dictator, I needed to be careful how advocacy of democracy was expressed and what was to be emphasized. It was fortunate that the columns were written in English and that the magazine had an international weight of its own. Therefore, I had considerable leeway in how and to what degree I expressed what I wanted say about Korea's democracy. Through these columns, I think I was able to give constructive advice not only to the government, but also to the opposition leaders, including Kim Young-sam and Kim Dae-jung. Writing regular columns gave me the opportunity to clarify my thoughts and arguments and to express them in a persuasive way. In addition, I think the *Newsweek* experience helped me to enhance my international name recognition.

Participating in Diplomacy

During the 1980s, I had the opportunity to participate in official and non-official conferences and projects as a representative of academia. I was also involved in government related activities in both advisory and delegate capacities. In 1985, Seoul and Pyongyang agreed to hold meetings between the two sides' Red Cross delegations for the purpose

Aspen Seminar, 1983

of arranging family reunions for those separated since the Korean War. It was puzzling that North Korea made the humanitarian gesture to allow the reunion of families, although the number was limited to 50, only two years after it killed 17 South Korean officials in an assassination attempt on the South Korean president's entourage in Burma (my brother in law Kim Jae-ik was one of the victims).

In 1985, over the course of arranging the family reunions, I participated in the negotiations as an advisor to the South Korean Red Cross and visited Pyongyang for the first time in that capacity. During my visit to North Korea, I was deeply disappointed and distressed that the suppressive atmosphere and hypocritical attitude of the officials were even more suffocating than I had imagined before the visit.

It was gratifying that we were able to arrange a limited number of family reunions. Unfortunately, however, because of the negative attitude of Pyongyang, we could not continue with this humanitarian project. There was no justifiable reason to block meetings and communication between the long separated family members, but North Korea would

Pyongyang Subway Ride, 1985

allow it only rarely and for political purposes, as if it was doing a big favor to the South or in return for some economic and political pay-off.

The Seoul Olympics were held in 1988, providing an opportunity to the government of newly elected president Roh Tae-woo to try what it called "*Nord Politik.*" This policy involved actively seeking diplomatic relations with Eastern European countries within the Soviet sphere of influence, and even the Soviet Union itself. In 1992, President Roh Tae-woo was able to normalize relations with China as well. In support of the government's policy to open and expand relations with countries in the communist bloc, there were efforts in the private and academic sectors to establish relations with counterparts in those countries.

Notably active in that respect among Korean university institutes were: the East-West Studies Institute of Yonsei University, the Sino-Soviet Institute of Hanyang University, and the Asiatic Research Center of Korea University. In recognition of their contribution to Korea's "*Nord Politik*" diplomacy, the organizations respective directors, Professor Kim Dal-choong of Yonsei University, Professor Yoo Se-hee of Hanyang University, and myself as the director of Korea University's

With a North Korean delegate, 1985

Asiatic Research Center each received a diplomatic medal of honor from the Roh Tae-woo government in December of 1992. Professor Kim's contribution to diplomacy toward the Eastern European countries, Professor Yoo's contribution to diplomacy toward the Soviet Union and China, and my contribution to diplomacy toward the United States, Japan, and other Asian countries were cited as reasons for our being awarded the diplomatic medal. For me, this series of activities likely must have served as the basis for my being appointed as the minister of foreign affairs in 1993. It also provided me with valuable experience and became an important asset when conducting the duties of the foreign minister.

During the final years of the 1980s and first two years of the 1990s, the world witnessed the unfolding of *perestroika* and *glasnost* in the Soviet Union, its subsequent disintegration, the fall of the Berlin Wall, and the reunification of Germany. As academics such as myself wrote columns and commentaries on these breathtaking developments on both ends of the Eurasian continent, we felt a strong sense of responsibility to understand the academic and policy implications of these events and

Filming for TV of removed wall between East and West Germany, 1990

accurately explain them to the Korean people.

I was also involved in making television specials with interviews from keen observers such as Henry Kissinger, Zbigniew Brzezinski, Paul Kennedy of Yale University, and Lester Thurow of MIT, as well as documentaries on the rebirth of Russia following the collapse of the Soviet Union and reunification of Germany. Those programs were well received by the viewers and were much talked about.

It was customary for academics of many countries to be engaged and involved in diplomacy and policy. Such activities were usually accepted as legitimate and useful. In Korea, however, because of the popular antagonism toward successive military governments, people generally had negative attitudes toward scholars and intellectuals participating in or cooperating with government activities. Fortunately, with democracy taking root in Korea in the 1990s, public negativity toward intellectual "engagement" in government had largely dissipated.

Chapter 3

A Young Minister

On January 18, 1993, I headed to Seoul's Gimpo Airport to catch a night plane to Manila in order to attend the Asia-Pacific Roundtable, which was to be held the next day. Dignitaries such as Philippine President Ramos were scheduled to attend. I arrived at the airport around 8:30 p.m. only to find that the airplane had already left. I had misread the departure time, confusing 20:00 for 10:00 p.m. The only choice I had was to turn around, go back home, and wait for the next day's plane.

After I returned home, I received an unexpected call from the personal secretary of then-president-elect Kim Young-sam, who had won the presidential election about a month earlier. The secretary, Kim Ki-sup, whom I had met before, told me that the president-elect would like to have dinner with me. He did not tell me what the meeting was about, but he made sure that I would come to Room 2209 of the Shilla Hotel on January 22nd.

I went to Manila the next day and attended the Asia-Pacific Roundtable. I still remember that President Ramos was giving instructions to his representatives who were negotiating with the rebels in Mindanao. President Ramos was talking to his aides while his guests, including me, were listening to the conversation (at least to Ramos' side of it). I was both taken aback and enticed by the informal way in which the Philippine president conducted this very serious business. At least it sounded as if the negotiations with the rebels were going well and the chances of a deal on government terms seemed high. That was good, I told myself. That will make the president jollier and the Phillippines more peaceful, at least for the time being. It also seemed to be a good omen for my meeting with our president-elect two days later.

When the dinner with President-elect Kim began on the appointed day, his television was already on. He was watching the news, which was covering the ongoing transition of power from the previous semi-military government to the incoming full-fledged civilian government. I do not remember talking about anything substantive or Mr. Kim asking me policy questions until the middle of the dinner when, suddenly, the president asked me whether I would be willing to work for him on foreign affairs (*oemu* in Korean). I was not expecting that he would offer me a job, but I was also prepared to say no in case he offered me a position as one of the secretaries in the Blue House.

"What do you mean, Mr. President-Elect?" I asked.

"I want you to be my minister of foreign affairs for five years," he said, "because I didn't like the practice of previous governments changing ministers every year or two."

I was dumbfounded. All I could meekly say was: "I am only a green-horn scholar. I have experience neither as a bureaucrat nor a politician. I am not sure if I can do it."

The president-elect declared: "I decide whether you are qualified or not. So you will take the job, but with one strict condition. You should not tell anyone about our conversation, not even your wife!"

When I came home, I was in full agony. Could I really do a job which I neither sought nor expected? How could I not tell my own wife what I heard from the president-elect, despite his forbidding it? On the other hand, what if I told my wife and nothing happens? Eventually, I told her about it, if only to spread the psychological burden between the two of us. Two weeks, then three weeks went by, and nothing. No communication whatsoever from the president-elect or his office. This was a time in Korea when no vetting, hearings, or parliamentary approval was required. But even if they had been required, how could the administration or parliament act on an appointment/designation that was never known or announced?

At the time, I was serving as a member of the academic advisory committee of the Ministry of Foreign Affairs. In that capacity, I was regularly receiving briefings from the leadership of the ministry, including the minister, on the issues and tasks that the ministry was facing. It made me realize how difficult and complex foreign policy issues were, particularly as they related to the North Korean nuclear program, relations with Japan, and the ongoing negotiations on market opening (particularly agriculture) within the context of the General Agreement on Tariffs and Trade (GATT) Uruguay Round.

I also realized that nearly all of the career ministry leadership (bureau directors and higher) were older than me. In Korea, age was still an important factor in government hierarchy. I was fifty-two at the time. Lacking the experience of a seasoned bureaucrat, I could not even imagine how difficult it would be to deal with the national assembly, other ministries and offices, the media, and members of the Blue House. Indeed, by appointing me, President-elect Kim Young-sam, who would be a novice in government himself, was taking a big, if calculated, chance, as it was almost unprecedented for a non-career diplomat to be appointed foreign minister. Although I would accept the job with a sense of mission and challenge, it was also true that the position was burdensome.

Because of the stern warning of the president-elect not to divulge it to anybody else, I did not have the opportunity to discuss the matter with my colleagues or those senior to me. Lee Hong-koo, with whom I would have been eager to talk, was serving as Korean ambassador to Britain. I finally spoke about it with Kim Kyong-won, a wise and experienced man who was a good friend of mine, who encouraged me to take the assignment, which he said was a good thing both for myself and the country.

More than a month passed between the job offer and actually assuming the office. However, I could not prepare myself for the work, as I was forbidden to discuss it with anyone, least of all, government and foreign ministry officials. As I was serving as an academic advisor to the foreign ministry, I tried to get as much information as possible about the policy issues and ministry personnel. However, I was not close to getting actual briefings from those responsible.

The inauguration of the new president took place on February 25th, 1993. Upon inauguration, he appointed as his senior advisor for diplomacy and security Professor Chung Chong-uk of Seoul National University, an academic colleague of mine. On the same day, the president appointed Mr. Hwang In-sung, former minister of transportation, as the prime minister. As the constitution stipulated that cabinet members were to be appointed at the recommendation of the prime minister, their names were to be announced the next day, on February 26th.

I did not attend the inauguration ceremony. At the time, the university was in winter recess. As the new cabinet was to be launched on February 26th, it would overlap with the beginning of the spring semester. Therefore, despite President Kim's order to keep silent on this matter, I felt I had the responsibility to give notice to the university president about my possible appointment as the foreign minister. As

February 25th happened to be the commencement day of the university, I made a personal visit to Professor Kim Hee-jip, the university president, after the commencement ceremony and informed him that I may not be able to return to the university for the spring semester. Professor Kim said he was delighted that I had been offered the position of foreign minister and congratulated me on it, even though I was unsure whether the appointment would actually be forthcoming.

Media Guessing Game

There was a keen interest in finding out who would become the leaders of each ministry. Until the afternoon of February 25th, there was no inkling of my appointment in the media reports. In the evening of that day, there were a few telephone calls from reporters about my joining the cabinet. My wife received the calls and replied that I was not available. However, a reporter from the *Segye Ilbo* by the name of Kook Ki-yon, rang our door bell around 1:00 a.m. on the 26th, which was close to the deadline to file the day's newspaper articles. I asked him to come in and led him into a room next to my study, in which I had drafted my inauguration speech. Kook asked me if I had received a telephone call from the Blue House. I said I had not, to which he asked me if I could cross my heart. I said I could because I had not received any phone calls from the Blue House. Mr. Kook seemed very disappointed and left our house dejected.

We turned on the TV on the morning of February 26th, as the names of new cabinet members would be announced at 9:00 a.m. Apparently, there was no leak regarding my appointment and no mention of my name prior to the official announcement. Television stations had to present my name without my portrait photo, as they had not anticipated

Appointment ceremony, February 1993

my name to be called.

About an hour after the announcement, I received a telephone call from the outgoing minister, Mr. Lee Sang-ok, who congratulated me and told me about the procedure regarding my official succession in the afternoon. Much of the morning was spent with receiving congratulatory telephone calls from acquaintances. At 2 p.m. an official car came from the ministry to drive me to the ministry for the inauguration ceremony.

When I arrived at the ministry, I found out that my inauguration speech was already prepared by the incumbent counselor to the minister, Yun Byung-se (later minister of foreign affairs). In the ceremony, I made the inauguration speech based on the draft I prepared at home, which emphasized the importance of preparing to deal with the three most urgent issues: the North Korean nuclear issue, Korea-Japan relations, and the Uruguay Round.

Transition into the Foreign Minister Position

Because I could not adequately prepare myself to become minister in advance, I decided to meet my predecessors *after* I assumed the office. I was told that, according to the usual practice, I was to meet my predecessors in the order of seniority. That is, I should meet the minister who had served the longest ago first and the most recent minister last. Although I followed this order, meeting my immediate predecessor at the end, I realized that this was a mistake, as it was necessary to meet him first for a smooth and orderly transition. I needed to talk with the latest minister as soon as possible.

In the foreign ministry, there are documents that are classified as "secret" in varying degrees from first to third. Before becoming the minister, my only experience in the government hierarchy was as a fifth level officer when I worked as a broadcaster in the government-run KBS radio station. Therefore, I was not familiar with secret classifications. I was wishing in vain to have some kind of instruction or orientation on what secret classification one, two, and three meant. It was hard to understand why there was no written or oral orientation regarding government procedures and secret classification.

Nor was there a built-in procedure for the handing over of work from one administration to the next. The only document that I received and had to sign the receipt contained lists of equipment and fixtures and nothing about policies or personnel matters.

The inadequate procedure for transition was even more pronounced in the presidential office since, unlike in a regular ministry, it was difficult to expect institutional or organizational memory to be handed down to the new administration from the outgoing officials. Thus, all the incoming administrators, including the president and ministers, were expected to learn by their wits and senses how to manage their duties.

No Solicitation for a Job, Please

There are many positions to rotate and fill in the foreign ministry—
ambassadors, bureau and section chiefs within the ministry, ministers and
counselors in the embassies abroad, administrative positions, etc. Before
my arrival, there were some ministers who were actively involved in the
personnel changes and there were others who were less involved. Also,
because of the relatively opaque nature of the administrations under
successive military governments, there used to be much interference in
personnel matters by politicians, the presidential office, and what were
known as "power" branches, such as the intelligence agency and the
military.

With the approval and explicit endorsement of the president, I made
it a firm policy of the ministry to make personnel decisions and changes
transparently, fairly, merit-based, and without outside interference. I
also tried to preserve the career diplomats' quota as much as possible.
In this process, I had to ask some of my close personal friends to come
back home from their posts abroad, even before their normal tour of
three years was up. I also admonished the diplomats not to rely on their
outside connections to promote their own career. I even threatened to
make the names public of those who asked for position favors through
their outside connections.

The president made it my exclusive responsibility to shuffle the
ambassadorial posts. There were two exceptions, however. He wanted
me to appoint Han Sung-soo, a former minister of commerce, as
ambassador to the United States and Mr. Hwang Byong-tae, a political
ally of his, as ambassador to one of the major countries, such as China
or Japan. I had no reason to object to these instructions of the president.
In fact, knowing them personally very well, I had every confidence that
they would do a good job as ambassadors in their respective posts.

In the foreign ministry, there were many senior officials who were several years older than me. As a graduate of an elite high school (Kyonggi High School) and Seoul National University (Department of Diplomacy), I had to make personnel decisions on individuals who were senior alumni of those schools. This was no easy task, as school ties were considered very important in Korea and graduates of my high school and college were of very high caliber in their own right.

I tried to make personnel decisions as fairly as possible. Curiously, when I assumed the ministership, a disproportionately large number of Kyonggi High School graduates were on the waiting list for assignment. Several of them were eventually assigned to European countries, which were considered rather favored posts. Although there was the impression (even criticism) that I was unduly favoring Kyonggi graduates, I could not reverse discriminate against them because I was also an alumnus of the school.

I was also asked to recommend someone for the post of vice-minister, for which I selected Ambassador Hong Soon-young, whom I was quite impressed with for his principled attitude and intellectual approach when he was serving as ambassador to Malaysia and Russia. Later, he became minister of foreign affairs and minister of unification under different administrations.

Stopping the U.S. from Bombing Yongbyun?

The most eventful thing to happen during my term as foreign minister took place on March 12, 1993, just two weeks after I assumed office. Around 10:30 a.m. in the morning, the director of the North American bureau, Chung Tae-ik, hurriedly came to my office and informed me that North Korea had formally declared it was withdrawing from the Nuclear Non-Proliferation Treaty (NPT).

I immediately called the Blue House to report this development to the president. However, I could not reach him, as he was attending the commencement ceremony of the Naval Academy in Chinhae on the southeastern coast. Eventually, I spoke with the president's chief of staff, Park Kwan-yong, and told him that I would provide a report to the president after his return to Seoul.

I summoned the leading members of the ministry and deliberated on how to respond to the North Korean action, which amounted to a serious provocation. We first discussed the implications of North Korea developing nuclear weapons. First, it increased the danger of armed conflict breaking out because regional countries might turn to more assertive actions to stop North Korea's nuclear development. Second, possession of nuclear weapons by North Korea would upend the balance of military power on the Korean Peninsula and would lead it to adopt a more aggressive policy toward the South. Third, it would motivate neighboring countries, including South Korea and Japan, to possess nuclear weapons themselves, leading to regional nuclear proliferation. Fourth, there was the danger of nuclear weapons and technology being transferred to rogue states and terrorist groups, further endangering regional and global security. Finally, North Korea's nuclear weapons development, without outside control or transparency, would risk large scale nuclear accidents. We concluded that it was important to closely coordinate with the United States and seek the cooperation of countries such as China and Russia, as well as international organizations like the United Nations and International Atomic Energy Administration (IAEA).

The issue that had prompted North Korea to withdraw from the NPT was the IAEA's demand to conduct a special inspection of its nuclear program, in light of the apparent discrepancy between the amount of

With President Clinton in the West Wing, the White House, 1994

plutonium that North Korea declared it had processed and the amount that the IAEA suspected that it actually had.

In the United States, the Clinton administration had been inaugurated only two months earlier and appointments to such key positions as Assistant Secretary of State for East Asia and the Pacific were barely arranged. The public reaction to North Korea's possible nuclear program was also intense, with some experts arguing that North Korea should be stopped with force if necessary.

This gave rise to the concern in South Korea about the possibility of impending military action by the United States against North Korea. The National Assembly and much of the media urged me to visit Washington as soon as possible and dissuade the United States from bombing Yongbyon, the location where North Korea reportedly was conducting its nuclear activities. I thought it was a legitimate, if overblown, concern and decided to make an early visit to Washington.

There was also an active debate within South Korea as to whether we should seek to resolve the issue through pressure or by negotiation. Another issue was the extent of South Korea's involvement in negotiations, should they take place. Also, if we sought to resolve the issue through negotiations, the end result would be a product of give and take, rather than a document of surrender. Hence, there arose the issue of what to give and what to take.

Among the government agencies closely involved in the issue, there was not a great deal of divergence over how to deal with North Korea. The Unification Ministry favored inter-Korea negotiation while the Foreign Ministry emphasized the need for close international (particularly U.S.) involvement. The National Security Planning Agency and Blue House took a somewhat harder line view than the Foreign Ministry. But it is fair to say that the Foreign Ministry took the lead in formulating a strategy, in coordination with the United States, to deal with the first North Korean nuclear crisis. The president's primary concern, in addition to the U.S. use of force, was whether South Korea would be seen as getting sidelined in the negotiations with North Korea.

In late March of that year (1993), I had a critical meeting with the Chinese Foreign Minister, Qian Qichen, at the Economic and Social Council for Asia and the Pacific (ESCAP) gathering held in Bangkok, Thailand. In that first of ten meetings I would have with him during my two-year term as foreign minister, I found Qian to be amiable, intelligent, and practical.

The most critical issue at hand was whether China, which was a member of the "permanent five" in the United Nations Security Council (UNSC), would allow the transfer of the issue from the IAEA to the UNSC. Since China had normalized its diplomatic relations with South Korea only a half year prior to the crisis, in August 1992, Beijing was feeling psychologically burdened towards North Korea. Therefore,

Beijing was hopeful that the U.S. would respond positively to the possibility of direct negotiations with North Korea.

Before heading to Bangkok for the meeting with the Chinese foreign minister, I dispatched our new director of the North American Bureau, Ambassador Jang Jae-ryong, to inform our American counterparts that I would try to induce China to bring the issue to the UNSC in return for the U.S. agreeing to negotiations with North Korea, if and when the opportunity arose. The United States approved of our proposed course, and eventually a quid-pro-quo deal was made with China in which the issue would be referred to the Security Council and a Washington-Pyongyang negotiation would be held.

During the last week of March, I visited Washington, D.C. for consultations with the Clinton administration. At the time, Winston Lord, a friend whom I had met when he was the president of the Council on Foreign Relations in New York, was designated as the Assistant Secretary of State for East Asia and the Pacific, but had not yet been confirmed by the Senate. In the course of my discussions with U.S. government officials such as Secretary of State Warren Christopher, Secretary of Defense Les Aspin, and National Security Advisor Anthony Lake, we came to a general understanding that we would seek to resolve the issue by bringing North Korea to the negotiating table rather than through the threat or use of force from the beginning.

Eventually, the issue was taken up by the UNSC and the U.S.-DPRK negotiation was held. However, it would take 19 months and many frustrating detours before an agreement (known as the Geneva Agreed Framework) was concluded in October 1994.

In this process, North Korea employed three tactics that can be seen as characteristic of its approach toward negotiations. One was brinkmanship, going to the edge of possible catastrophe before turning around for a breakthrough. For example, in January 1994, Pyongyang withdrew its spent fuel rods from its five-megawatt (MW) reactor and started to reprocess them for plutonium production, intensifying conflict with the United States and its allies. Their second tactic was to frontload small and seemingly insignificant concessions in the earlier stages of the negotiations and backload large and significant measures at a later stage. This was to avoid making irretrievable concessions early and to enable itself to restore the status quo if the negotiation was not satisfactory. The third tactic was so-called "salami tactics," by which North Korea would slice the measures and concessions into several thin pieces under such slogans as "action for action." This was to prevent a comprehensive resolution of an issue in one big sweep.

Interests of Nations Related to Negotiations with North Korea

The United States did not hesitate to take the leading role in stopping the North Korean nuclear program, as it threatened not only the security of the Korean Peninsula, but also nuclear nonproliferation efforts. Using a road map agreed upon with South Korea, the Clinton administration decided to attempt a resolution of the issue by dialogue and negotiation rather than use of force.

South Korea, which had the most to lose by North Korea becoming a nuclear weapons state and was most vulnerable to North Korean threats and provocations, probably had the least leverage vis-à-vis North Korea to force it to abandon the program. Under such circumstances, the only choice for South Korea was to work closely with the international community, especially the United States, to persuade, cajole, or force North Korea to come to terms with the rest of the world on the nuclear issue.

Japan, the second most threatened country after South Korea,

At the White House, with Vice President Al Gore, January 1994

With Russian President Boris Yeltsin, 1993

came to the table without much of a voice at the beginning but soon gained influence, as it was bearing a considerable share of the financial burden in the construction of the North's light-water reactors (LWRs). It was agreed that energy assistance would be provided to North Korea in the form of shipments of heavy fuel oil and the building of light-water reactors, as part of the Geneva Agreed Framework. In exchange, Pyongyang promised to give up the development of its nuclear weapons program. South Korea and the United States coordinated closely with Japan during the negotiation process, as Japan demonstrated a high level of interest in the resolution of the issue. Thus, when the negotiation took place, even though it was outwardly conducted between the United States and North Korea, both South Korea and Japan were closely involved through coordination with the United States.

As for Russia, since the North Korean nuclear issue emerged after the Soviet Union dissolved and the Russian Federation was formed under the leadership of Boris Yeltsin, the country held a rather favorable attitude toward South Korea and cooperated with the resolution. Each time I visited Moscow as South Korea's foreign minister, I had friendly and helpful exchanges with President Yeltsin. Although there were no multilateral talks on the North Korean nuclear issue (the Six-Party Talks would not begin until the early 2000s), as a permanent member of the U.N. Security Council and still a nominal ally of North Korea with a mutual defense treaty, Russia could play a useful and constructive role in terms of intelligence and diplomatic persuasion.

China, considering their close proximity to North Korea, would be directly threatened by North Korean nuclear weapons, and therefore had to oppose its nuclear program. At the same time, however, China also had an interest in keeping the North Korean regime afloat and preventing an armed conflict on the Korean Peninsula. Therefore, China refrained from applying maximum pressure on North Korea to give up its nuclear

With Chinese Foreign Minister Qian Qichen

program. However, at critical moments when China's firm action was needed (as in June 1994), China did play a constructive role in bringing North Korea away from the brink and returning to the table.

The June 1994 crisis began in April of that year, when Pyongyang withdrew 8,000 of its used nuclear fuel rods for processing. On June 13th, it formally announced its withdrawal from the IAEA, following its declaration of withdrawal from the Nuclear Non-Proliferation Treaty (NPT) in March 1993. The IAEA announced that the North Korean action effectively erased the possibility of ascertaining North Korea's past nuclear activities or measuring the amount of North Korean fissile material production. The North Korean nuclear issue thus became a target of U.N. Security Council sanctions. North Korea declared that such sanctions by the U.N. would be construed as an act of war. The United States responded with military augmentation in Korea, including the dispatch of an aircraft carrier to the East Sea. There was speculation about possible U.S. bombing of Yongbyon, the North Korean nuclear site, and war clouds hung low over the Korean Peninsula.

In early June, as a sanctions vote loomed in the U.N. Security Council, I visited Beijing for meetings with Foreign Minister Qian Qichen and Vice Minister in charge of Asian affairs, Tang Jiaxuan. I had an in-depth discussion with both of them on the North Korean nuclear issue. In the meetings, I emphasized that China had to let Pyongyang know in advance that Beijing was not prepared to exercise a veto of U.N. sanctions on its nuclear program.

On the way to the airport after the meetings, Vice-Minister Tang Jiaxuan, who was also riding in the same car, asked me if I could elaborate on my suggestion about Beijing's warning to North Korea. I thought this was an implicit acknowledgment that Beijing was, in fact, seriously considering such an option. I told Tang that, as North Korea was indeed afraid of such a resolution, this message by China to Pyongyang was likely to make it reconsider its brinkmanship and help bring it back to the table.

On June 12th, a few days after I returned to Seoul, the Chinese ambassador in Seoul, Chang Tingwen called me "on an urgent matter" and informed me in a "non-paper" format about instructions he received from Beijing. Ambassador Chang told us the following: "On June 10, 1994, the Chinese Vice Minister, Tang Jiaxuan, notified the North Korean ambassador in Beijing about China's position regarding the current deadlock on the North Korean nuclear issue.

First, China is unhappy about North Korea's withdrawal of spent fuel rods from the five-megawatt reactor.

Second, China was no longer able to defend North Korea, in view of its actions regarding its nuclear program.

Third, China wants North Korea to exhibit greater flexibility on the issue. In the absence of which, China would not be able to prevent the passage of a sanctions resolution in the UN Security Council.

Finally, China strongly urges North Korea to change its attitude."

Such a strong and direct message from the Chinese government must have been a considerable shock to Pyongyang, which subsequently invited former U.S. President Jimmy Carter to Pyongyang to meet the North Korean president, Kim Il-sung. Upon receiving the Chinese ambassador's "non-paper" message, we immediately relayed it to the U.S. government and subsequently to the Japanese government.

Assuming that the Chinese were truthful in notifying us about their actions vis-à-vis North Korea (and I had no reason to believe otherwise), China played a critical and constructive role to persuade Pyongyang to modify its attitude toward the United States on the nuclear issue. In effect, Beijing was notifying Pyongyang that it had better shape up, or else China would no longer shield North Korea.

Behind former President Carter's June 1994 visit to North Korea was the persistent effort of the U.S. ambassador in Seoul, James L. Laney. Before taking the ambassadorial post in Korea, Ambassador Laney was the president of Emory University in Atlanta, Georgia. The university had long established ties with the Carter Center. He was in close contact with former President Carter, and before Carter's trip to Pyongyang in June 1994, Ambassador Laney and I talked about the possibility of his visit to North Korea in connection with the nuclear crisis. For North Korea, Carter's visit must have been seen as a way out of the dilemma it was facing, in light of Beijing's warning to "change your behavior, or else."

Although many people in South Korea had misgivings about President Carter's visit to Pyongyang, I thought it was one way for North Korea to adopt a conciliatory attitude while still saving face. I discussed the subject with President Kim Young-sam, who accepted my suggestion that we make the most of the situation by using President Carter's visit

Carter's meeting with Kim Il-sung in Pyongyang, June 1994

as a means to deliver a message to Kim Il-sung for a summit meeting between the presidents of North and South Korea.

President Carter visited Seoul on his way to and from Pyongyang. As South Korea's Foreign Minister, I met Mr. Carter both times before his meetings with President Kim Young-sam. At a luncheon meeting before Carter's visit, President Kim asked him to convey the message to Kim Il-sung that he was willing to meet with the North Korean leader directly, even in Pyongyang.

President Carter came back from Pyongyang with two messages. One was that North Korea was willing to resume talks with the United States over resuming IAEA inspections of North Korean nuclear sites and the possibility of stopping its nuclear program. The other was that President Kim Il-sung was willing to have a summit meeting with President Kim Young-sam.

Did South Korea Stop the United States from Bombing North Korea?

How close the Korean Peninsula came to war in June 1994 was a point of debate in South Korea for several years. Many believed that

Meeting with Secretary of Defense William Perry, Washington, D.C., 1994

the United States was close to conducting a preventive strike on North Korea, thus possibly precipitating a second Korean War. In 1999, former President Kim Young-sam even claimed that he personally stopped the United States from bombing Yongbyun by talking President Clinton out of it in a telephone call.[7]

However, President Kim's claim was, at best, exaggerated. There is no record that I know of, for such a telephone call in June 1994. Furthermore, according to then U.S. Secretary of Defense William Perry, although there was a contingency plan regarding the bombing of Yongbyun, it remained shelved and was not even shown to President Clinton. This statement stands in contrast to the view that the contingency plan received Clinton's approval. Also, it is highly unlikely that the United States would have failed to consult South Korea in advance if it was about to carry out such a plan.

---

7   Kim Young-sam, *Memoirs of President Kim Young-sam [Kimyeongsam daetongryeongui hoegorok]*, vol. 1, Seoul, 2002, p.315

What alarmed some Koreans, including President Kim, was that, in addition to military augmentation in and around the Korean Peninsula, the United States was conducting non-combatant evacuation operation (NEO) drills. However, these moves were intended to demonstrate the U.S.' resolve to press North Korea as far as possible, rather than as preparation for an actual attack on North Korea.

New York Times
A Korean Voice: Forceful, but Almost Inaudible

By DAVID E. SANGER, Special to The New York Times

December 28, 1993

SEOUL, South Korea, Dec. 21 – Not long ago a military officer here, a hard-liner when it comes to North Korea's nuclear bomb project, expressed some grudging admiration for how the negotiations with the North had been handled by South Korea's very unmilitary Foreign Minister, Han Sung Joo.

Mr. Han, he said, is a brilliant man, the country's premier political scientist, probably a pretty crafty negotiator. But he suffers a character flaw, the officer said: he is so soft-spoken, so calm, that "he makes me wonder if he is really Korean."

In his Foreign Ministry office the other day, the man who has emerged as the precise, English-speaking voice of a new South Korea, one whose Government is no longer dominated by former military officials, conceded that he had often asked himself the same question.

"I'm more like a Thai than a Korean," the 53-year-old former professor said with a wan smile, in a voice so quiet that visitors sometimes have to lean over to hear him.

"I think I'd like to do things in a more rational way, in a country that you could call, well, emotion-prone."

Chief Architect of Strategy

Amid considerable struggles within South Korea's year-old Government, the first headed by a civilian in three decades, Mr. Han has emerged as the chief architect of Seoul's and sometimes Washington's strategy for dealing with the Communist Government of Kim Il Sung.

Along the way, he has brought a new tone to his country's diplomatic efforts, a self-assurance that has permitted the South to treat its traditional enemy less like a mortal threat, and more like a cranky, sometimes unpredictably violent old relative who must be humored and negotiated with in his last days.

In a diplomatic role reversal, it has often been Mr. Han, sitting within firing range of North Korea's forces along the demilitarized zone, who has urged the Clinton Administration, in distant Washington, to calm down, to keep cajoling and tempting North Korea's leaders rather than threatening them.

He is acknowledged as the architect of what has come to be known as the "package deal," the current offer to trade full inspection of the North's declared nuclear sites in return for an end to the annual Team Spirit military exercises and talks about trade, aid and diplomatic recognition.

But in Seoul, Mr. Han, who had never before served in a senior Government post, makes many uncomfortable—especially in the military and the intelligence agencies. "The truth is that I have had an easier time dealing with the barbarians than my own domestic audience," he acknowledged, smiling at his use of a label once reserved for all foreigners.

The Center of Gravity

"An overwhelming thought here is that we cannot trust the North Koreans, and therefore, there is no use in talking to them. There is much truth in that. But they don't understand that on the basis of this possible deceit it is still useful to go on talking."

To Washington's frustration, South Korea's language has often seemed to veer from hawkish to accommodating in recent months, as different factions in Seoul captured the ear of President Kim Young Sam. But the center of gravity returns regularly to Mr. Han's let's-keep-negotiating view, one that a former official here says won the day because Mr. Han "nudged, pushed, cajoled, waited and let others take credit."

Mr. Han understands the price of failure: he still carries a small piece of shrapnel in his lower back, a stray bit of allied fire left over from September 1950, when Gen. Douglas MacArthur's troops retook Seoul. He may have been saved, he said, by a North Korean soldier who "took out a long cloth and tied up my wound," as he escaped to the mountain house of a family friend.

A few days later, caught again in the crossfire, he and his parents narrowly escaped execution by a less friendly band of North Koreans, who let them go after his father deceived them about the family's true loyalties.

Unlike those of many in his generation, though, Mr. Han's views seem shaped less by the trauma of the war than by the two decades he spent out of Korea starting in the early 1960's -- a sojourn of study and teaching that wound through the campuses of Berkeley, the City University of New York and Columbia University.

'Quietness is Deceiving'

He quickly became the best-known Korean in the American foreign policy circuit, and grew close to many of the people who have since become the core of the Clinton Administration's foreign policy team. But by the time he returned to South Korea in the early 1980's as a professor, critic and columnist -- he often wrote for *Newsweek*'s international editions -- his views were frequently unwelcome here.

"His quietness is deceiving, because he is quite firm," said Lee Hong Ku, the former Minister of Unification and a longtime friend of Mr. Han. "Clearly past Governments were not happy with his calls for democracy. But the way he presented his case, and his international status, seemed to protect him."

His selection as Foreign Minister this year was a surprise: as an academic, he had often taken the minority view here that relations with North Korea were not zero-sum, that the North could get some of the economic development it desperately seeks without harming the South's interests. It is a view he still holds.

But in his move from "a practical scholar to a scholarly practitioner," he said, he has decided that most of the international relations works he keeps on his shelves "are not really relevant" in dealing with a nuclear renegade.

An Evolving Viewpoint

The exception, he said, is "The Strategy of Conflict," a classic written by Thomas C. Schelling, the Harvard professor. "Not a day passes without my thinking of some of Schelling's examples," he said, declining to tip his hand by citing a few. (Curiously, Mr. Han's critics cite the book as well, noting its warning that in a crisis the side that is too controlled, too disciplined and too sensitive to counterarguments can lose the respect of its opponents.)

Now, Mr. Han says, his own view of North Korea is evolving considerably. Though North Korea is autocratic, he said, "it may not have a very monolithic decision-making structure." And that opens it up to divisions, giving the South a chance to dangle incentives.

"It's worth a try," he said. "Nothing will persuade the hard-liners like success."

A version of this *New York Times* article appeared in print on December 28, 1993.

The "What If…" Question

Despite the Clinton administration's lukewarm attitude towards Carter's visit to Pyongyang, it nevertheless transformed the situation in two ways. One was the agreement to hold an inter-Korean summit. The other was the resumption of stalled negotiations on the nuclear issue between the United States and North Korea.

When Carter returned to Seoul from Pyongyang on the morning of June 18th, I met him at the American ambassador's residence, where he told me that Kim Il-sung had accepted President Kim Young-sam's offer to hold a summit meeting. I reported the message to President Kim immediately afterwards, as he was supposed to have lunch with the former U.S. president. Carter was then scheduled to have a press conference at 4:00 p.m. regarding his visit to Pyongyang.

We wanted to make sure that the announcement concerning the inter-Korean summit was to be made by the South Korean government rather than Carter. Thus, we announced the news around 2:00 p.m. Subsequently, a follow-up negotiation between the unification ministers of North and South Korea agreed to hold the summit meeting on July 25th. Regrettably, Kim Il-sung died of a heart attack on July 7th, and the inter-Korean summit could not take place. We do not know what could have been accomplished if the summit had been held. The one thing we know is that President Kim Young-sam, prior to the ill-fated summit, was confident that he could draw concessions out of Kim Il-sung so that the North Korean nuclear program would be stopped and the two Koreas could move closer to reunification.

The U.S.-North Korea negotiations resumed in Geneva, Switzerland, following President Carter's visit to Pyongyang and the death of Kim Il-sung. After almost three months of intensive talks, the Geneva Agreed Framework was concluded. The Agreed Framework was not a document of surrender and thus contained provisions which reflected the logic of give and take. The negotiation was conducted by representatives of the United States and North Korea, and South Korea was effectively a third-party negotiator in the meeting, as the United States closely consulted with us during all phases of the negotiation process.

North Korea agreed to freeze all of its nuclear activities and facilities, and to come into "full compliance" with IAEA safeguards when a "significant portion of the LWR project is completed". It also promised to dismantle its nuclear facilities and material at the moment when the core parts of the light-water reactors were to be delivered. North Korea was also to remain a member of the Nuclear Non-Proliferation Treaty (NPT) and the International Atomic Energy Agency (IAEA) and allow IAEA monitoring of its nuclear facilities. After much wrangling and considerable delay, Pyongyang agreed to hold a North-South Korean dialogue.

In return, the United States, in cooperation with South Korea and other countries, would build two 2000 megawatt LWRs, with the expenses to be paid by long-term loans provided to North Korea. The United States also pledged that it would not attack North Korea militarily, provide 500,000 tons of heavy oil per year, and establish diplomatic relations with North Korea.

Looking back, it can be said that the Agreed Framework had both merits and demerits. It was faulted by critics for failing to deal satisfactorily with the IAEA complaints. They were quick to note that the agreement allowed several years to pass before the IAEA could conduct "special inspections" of the undeclared nuclear waste site. Additionally, it has been argued that the agreement "rewarded" North Korea with benefits, such as a new energy supply and LWRs, for its defiance of the IAEA.

On the positive side, the agreement put an end to the crisis, which could have brought about a destructive military clash. It also succeeded in freezing the North Korean nuclear program and activities, effectively ending its plutonium-based nuclear weapons program. Finally, it gave North Korea a stake in implementing the agreement. The prospect of receiving heavy fuel oil and securing LWRs gave Pyongyang an incentive to "behave," at least for several years.

North Korea kept its nuclear program frozen, allowed the IAEA to continue inspections of its nuclear facilities, and had the fuel rods from its old nuclear reactor withdrawn and encased for safekeeping. There is no question that the relatively restrained behavior of North Korea until 2002 can be attributed to the Geneva Agreement with the United States.

Was the Geneva Agreed Framework of 1994 a failure? We know North Korea cheated, but was it because the agreement itself was at fault? We do not know if North Korea planned to have a clandestine nuclear program when it signed the 1994 Agreed Framework. What we do know is that, around 1997-1998, when the time was nearing for it to dismantle its nuclear facilities in accordance with the agreement, it found an opportunity to pursue its nuclear program by using highly enriched uranium (HEU). Then in 2002 to 2003, it also found an excuse to scrap the agreement and openly restart its nuclear program.

So there are valid criticisms of the Agreed Framework, as well as valid arguments for why it was successful, at least in part. It is clear, however, that since resuming its nuclear activities in earnest in 2003, North Korea has greatly improved its nuclear weapons program, both in terms of scale and capability. North Korea may have developed nuclear weapons regardless of the international community's actions. Yet, in my view, there are two instances which inadvertently contributed to North Korea's march toward becoming a nuclear weapons state. Both cases have something to teach us today.

One is the 1992 attempt to force a "special inspection" of North Korea's nuclear facilities after the IAEA discovered a "discrepancy" between the amount of plutonium North Korea admitted to have processed and the amount the IAEA suspected they had produced. The other was the 2002 attempt to probe the North Korean uranium enrichment program after it was discovered. In the first case, we placed more emphasis on probing the North's past activities rather than maintaining the current inspection regime. In the second case, we placed more emphasis on the *future* of the North Korean nuclear program instead of curtailing their capabilities at the time.

My point is that, without ignoring or tolerating their past or potential future infringements, we could have handled the cases differently. In 1992, we insisted too much on "special inspections" aimed at clarifying the "discrepancy" of plutonium production. In 2002, we could have handled the uranium enrichment issue without dismantling the Geneva agreement. The former would have risked the present and future in order to probe the past, and the latter would have risked the present in order to prevent future danger.

Preventing War

As I did not seek to become foreign minister, I did not have any particular plans as to how I would conduct myself in the position. However, only two weeks after I assumed office, the North Korean nuclear crisis broke and became the most urgent issue I had to deal with during my tenure. For the next 19 months, I had to wrestle with the question of war and peace until the crisis was finally resolved in October, 1994.

Even though there was no set term for a cabinet minister, I was determined that, during my tenure, I would prevent the outbreak of war on the Korean Peninsula and somehow settle the North Korean nuclear issue. On the basis of discussions with my staff advisors and U.S. counterparts, I decided that it would be useful and necessary to draw a roadmap of how to approach the problem.

According to this roadmap, we would try to resolve the issue through dialogue and negotiation as much as possible. The use of force would be the very last resort, to be considered only after all other means and avenues had been tried and exhausted. In this effort, South Korea and the United States would coordinate their efforts closely and mobilize the support of other concerned countries, primarily Japan, as well as China and Russia.

Ultimately, events generally progressed along the lines of the roadmap, even though we had to experience war scares along the way. Although North Korea violated the Agreed Framework in the late 1990s by secretly engaging in a uranium enrichment program, I do not think the Geneva agreement can be faulted for this transgression. In fact, I believe North Korea would have inevitably sought a clandestine and alternate route to nuclear weapons development after the plutonium route was blocked by the Agreed Framework.

In South Korea, many of those who had misgivings about the Geneva agreement eventually came to regard it positively, even telling me that they had been mistaken to have opposed the agreement before. North Korea decided to "cheat" when it reached the point, according to the agreement, that it was necessary to abandon and dismantle all its nuclear facilities and materials. In this regard, one can argue that the Agreed Framework was ultimately scrapped because of its effectiveness and success.

Robert Gallucci, who negotiated the Geneva Agreed Framework in 1994, authored a book with his colleagues Joel S. Wit and Daniel B. Poneman under the title, *Going Critical: The First North Korean Nuclear Crisis* (Washington, D.C., Brookings Institution Press, 2004). In the signing page, he wrote the following message for me: "If it were not for you, your hard work, integrity and commitment to resolve the crisis, there would not have been an Agreed Framework. You have the thanks and admiration of all the members of this book, and my appreciation for your friendship, Bob Gallucci, April, 2004."

Hand-shake with Japanese Prime Minister Morihiro Hosokawa, 1993

A Relationship That Is Close and Afar

In my inauguration speech, one of the three major foreign policy issues I discussed was Korea's relations with Japan, in addition to the North Korean nuclear issue and the ongoing Uruguay Round on trade.

While focusing on the North Korean nuclear issue, I also had to address the other two issues. Korea suffered under Japan's colonial rule for 35 years until the end of the Second World War. Even after the two geographically close but temperamentally distant countries normalized their diplomatic relations in 1965, the relationship continued to stumble over a number of issues. Such issues included the ownership of an uninhabited island, Koreans' belief that Japan inadequately acknowledged and repented over its harsh rule of Korea, supposed distortion of historical facts in Japanese textbooks, and Japan's failure to accept responsibility for what is known euphemistically as wartime "comfort women."

There was a time in the late 1980s when the bilateral relations between Japan and Korea looked rather hopeful. Korea hosted the Seoul Olympics in 1988 and Koreans were happy and confident. Japan seemed to respect Korea's achievements. They seemed to be building a mutually beneficial relationship that would wash away the past and make good neighbors out of the two nations.

However, as the issue of comfort women surfaced, Korean victims who had been reluctant to appear in public began to openly testify about their suffering. Dozens of women's organizations got together in a show of solidarity to represent and advocate for the honor and interests of the victims. They campaigned for the issue beyond simple bilateral relations between Korea and Japan and turned it into an international campaign on "war and women's rights."

As a result of their efforts, international organizations such as the U.N. Commission on Human Rights and Committee on the Elimination of Discrimination Against Women, as well as parliaments of several countries including the United States, Canada, and the Netherlands, adopted resolutions condemning sexual slavery in wartime and calling for restitution for the victims. As those who had been mobilized to serve as comfort women were passing away from old age, there was increasing urgency to resolve the issue.

But in the early 1990s, Korea and Japan had distinct views on the comfort women issue. Japan held the view that all claims, including those related to wartime comfort women, had been resolved with the 1965 agreement on Korea's pre-World War II property claims against Japan. On the other hand, Korea argued that this was not a matter that could be settled within the context of property claims. Rather, Korea contended, the resolution of the issue should start with Japan's admission of government involvement in and responsibility for comfort women issues. Japan took the position that wartime comfort women had been recruited and mobilized by private parties and therefore the government could not be held responsible. However, in October 1991, documents were found in the library of the Japanese Self Defense Agency (later Ministry of Defense) that indicated government involvement in control of the comfort women. After this revelation, Chief Cabinet Secretary Koichi Kato, who also served as the government's spokesperson, recognized the Japanese government's responsibility by stating that "there was no denying the involvement of the Japanese Army in the comfort women operation."

When I became the Korean foreign minister, the issue was still unresolved. We made it clear that the most important action that the Japanese government should take is to officially acknowledge the Japanese government's wartime control and operation of the comfort women project and take necessary measures to address the damage suffered by the victims.

Newsweek

Asia's Distant Neighbors by Han Sung-Joo

AUGUST 31, 1992

Though neither will admit it, Japan and Korea are both to blame for the tensions between them.

When Korean marathoner Hwang Young-cho crossed the finish line first in Barcelona this month, he became an instant national hero back home. But what thrilled Koreans was not so much his victory, which gave South Korea its 12th gold medal of the Olympics. No, the real reason was that he beat the Japanese contender. Hwang's feat enabled Koreans to wash away the ignominy of another Korean marathoner who won the Olympic gold medal 56 years earlier. No Korean will soon forget or forgive the fact that Sohn Kee-jong, the Korean marathon winner in Berlin, had to run with the

Japanese flag on his chest.

What made the marathon victory over Japan so sweet to many Koreans was the fact that it came at a time when the relationship between the two Asian neighbors has soured considerably. Indeed, this may be the low point in the relationship since the restoration of diplomatic ties in 1965. Even more worrisome, unlike past years when the sparring was mainly between governments, the public in both countries, particularly the intellectuals and the media, has now entered the ring.

The Koreans and the Japanese are still fighting the Second World War almost half a century after it was over. Koreans say that Japan is prolonging the war by not disclosing, much less teaching, the truth about the past. As evidence of Japan's insincerity, they cite its effort to cover up the case of Korean "comfort women" who were forced to provide sex to Japanese troops during the war. To Koreans, Japan's failure to confront its past may be as unforgivable as what the Japanese did to the Koreans before 1945.

For their part, the Japanese put the blame for the continuing quarrel on Korean emotionalism and obstinacy. "We have apologized enough," they say. "How many more times must we say we are sorry?" They say they are tired of Koreans blaming Japan for their own problems—such as the trade deficit, the economic slowdown and inability to improve North and South Korean relations. Korea needs Japan more than Japan needs Korea. Hence, they advise, it would be best for Koreans if they turned their eyes to the future and cooperated with Japan rather than nitpicking over old issues. If this is how some Japanese felt before, they have kept such sentiments to themselves without expressing them in public. But now, mainstream journals and newspapers routinely publish articles that betray an attitude that the Japanese call *kenkan* (hating Korea).

How is it that, 47 years after the end of the Japanese rule and 27 years after the normalization of diplomatic relations, the two nations can be so at odds? For 400 years since the Hideyoshi invasion of Korea, there has been no love lost between these two proud and energetic peoples. Although Japan moved ahead of Korea through early modernization in the 19th century, and ruled over Korea for 35 years in the 20th century, Koreans never accepted nor recognized Japan's "superiority." It is true that Koreans tend to cling to the issues of the past longer and more persistently than Japan's other neighbors, who were also victims of its aggression. But that is because the Japanese rule was harsher in Korea and left deeper psychic wounds. Only the appearance of genuine repentance and unconditional admission of guilt would have elicited Korean forgiveness.

Such, however, would have been a totally unrealistic expectation. Unlike Germany, where wartime crimes could be blamed on Hitler's Nazi regime, Japan kept the emperor in whose name the war and its colonialist policies were pursued. Japan never felt guilty: the only regret was that it lost. Japan would apologize only if its victims demanded it—and then only to appease them. For the Koreans as well as other Asian victims of Japanese aggression, it was a futile exercise to demand a "sincere" apology from Japan.

Past guilt: What Koreans have failed to recognize and accept is that repentance can only be a voluntary act. If Japan does not accept its guilt, it is primarily Japan's own problem. If moral persuasion is not possible, political pressure will only backfire. Korea should let Japan deal with its own conscience. Koreans have also to recognize that, half a century after the departure of Japan, it is not the same generation of guilty Japanese from whom they are seeking psychological remedy. Even in a society of geriatric elites like Japan, those who make important decisions are now of the post-World War II generation. In all probability, Kiichi Miyazawa will be the last Japanese prime minister who has an adult memory of prewar Japan. Most active Japanese today do not associate themselves with, much less feel responsible for, what their elders once did. It is too bad that Japan could not be made to accept its past guilt and responsibility earlier. It would do no good to push them now.

To be sure, the practical issues, such as the Japanese Peacekeeping Operations bill and trade imbalance, do get in the way of constructive bilateral relations. The former gives Koreans jitters of a Japanese military revival; the latter makes them resentful of Japan. But it is more the symbolic and emotional issues of the past that provide the fuel for the ill will between the two nations.

Ultimately, the leaders of both countries must recognize the roots of the problem and deal with them. Either for lack of vision or courage, the political and intellectual elite in both countries have refused to buck popular sentiments. The Japanese leaders could have been, indeed should have been, more resolute and forthright in accepting the responsibilities of the past. The Korean leaders have failed to warn the people of the consequences of their uncalculating emotions.

The Korea-Japan relationship was at its best in 1988 when Korea hosted the Seoul Olympics. Koreans were happy and confident; Japan showed respect for Korea's achievements. It is not another apology by Japan but a visible effort on its part to cooperate in building a happy and confident Korea that will help wash away the past and make good neighbors out of the two nations.

To the credit of the outgoing Japanese government of Prime Minister Kiichi Miyazawa, Japan issued an official statement admitting the government's role in the operation of the comfort women project in the form of a "statement by the Chief Cabinet Secretary Yohei Kono" issued on August 4, 1993. In the statement, the Japanese government acknowledged that the Japanese army was directly and indirectly involved in organizing and managing the comfort women, that a large portion of them were taken from the Korean Peninsula, and that, on the whole, the recruitment, transportation, and management were done by coercion and against the victims' will. The statement also expressed an apology and repentance, claiming that Japan would use the case as a lesson to learn from history.

The "Kono Statement", as it was known in both Korea and Japan, was not 100 percent satisfactory from the Korean point of view.

Meeting with Japanese Foreign Minister Yohei Kono, 1994

However, our government considered it was as far as the Japanese government could go in admitting Japan's misdeeds during the war and apologizing for the pain that had been inflicted on the victims. As for financial restitution, the Kim administration's view was that, even though it neither expected nor demanded government-to-government compensation, it was urging Japan to address the victims' wish to have their honor restored and financial compensation achieved by way of government funding.

However, the Japanese government, instead of making a direct payment to the former comfort women, chose to disburse funds through a non-governmental funding campaign called "Citizens' Fund for Asian Peace to Support Women," thus inciting opposition and protest from the victims themselves and Korean women's organizations operating on behalf of their honor and interests. As the issue dragged on without a resolution, the Korean Constitutional Court ruled in August 2011 that the Korean government was negligent in its duties for not trying harder to resolve the issue of the former comfort women's rightful demands.

After five more years of back and forth between the two countries, Japan and Korea put an end to the dispute in December 2015 with a bilateral agreement. Japan stated that "The issue of comfort women, with the involvement of the Japanese military authorities at that time, was a grave affront to the honor and dignity of large numbers of women, and the Government of Japan is painfully aware of responsibilities from this perspective." The Japanese government also agreed to provide a fund (about 1 billion yen) for the elderly comfort women, along with an apology by Japan's prime minister and the admission of "deep responsibility" for the issue.

Such an "agreement" elicited two opposing reactions among the Korean public. On one hand, those who were worried about the deteriorating relationship between Korea and Japan, at a time when the two countries had to cooperate closely to deal with the North Korean nuclear threat, felt relieved by the apparent show of reconciliation and welcomed the agreement. On the other hand, citizens' organizations such as Solidarity on the Comfort Women Problem and many of the victims themselves expressed a strong sense of dissatisfaction over the inadequacy of Japanese apology and repentance.

The Uruguay Round and Opening of the Rice Market

The third major issue that I faced as foreign minister was how to deal with the problems of the Uruguay Round (UR), which was nearing the end of negotiations and bringing with it the opening of the agricultural market. The Uruguay Round had begun in 1986 in the renowned resort town of Punta del Este in southern Uruguay. Since then, a series of negotiations among trading countries had taken place to promote trade and lower tariffs by revising the General Agreement on Trade and Tariffs (GATT) that had gone into effect in 1948.

Included in the UR negotiations was the issue of opening the manufacturing and agricultural markets. Korea had much to gain by mutually lowering barriers and tariffs on manufacturing products but much to lose by trade agreements on agricultural products, due to its weak competitiveness in that area. Thus, strong opposition emerged to the opening of the agricultural market, particularly rice, as the deadline for the negotiations neared in late 1993. During the campaign for president in 1992, President Kim Young-sam pledged that, if elected, he would block the opening of the rice market, placing his office on the line.

In the course of negotiating to become a member of the UR system, the administration realized that they had no choice but to open the rice market in some form. They agonized over how to reconcile the requirements of joining the new trading system with domestic political demands. The final negotiation for the opening of the rice market was under the purview of the Ministry of Agriculture. Minister Huh Shin-haeng, before leaving for Geneva where the final negotiation was being held, resolutely declared at the airport, "I would give my neck in order to block the rice market opening."

One of Five "Culprits"

In the end, in order to enter the new global system, later named the World Trade Organization (WTO), Korea decided to accept what is known as MMA (Minimum Market Access), by which the tariffication of rice imports would receive a reprieve for ten years in return for a minimum percentage of access to the Korean rice market that would be increased every year of the period of reprieve. That meant that another round of negotiation would be necessary at the end of 2004. At this turn of events, the rice farmers and organizations who had opposed the opening of the Korean market felt a strong sense of betrayal by the government's action and named five government officials, including the prime minister, the minister of agriculture, the minister of foreign affairs, and two others as the "five culprits of the 1994 concession to foreign pressure." Thus, I became one of the nation's "culprits" because the Foreign Ministry was closely involved in the UR negotiating process.

As is the case with many trade-related issues, the opening of the rice market had both political and economic significance. Farmers occupied only seven percent of the Korean population, and the rice growers were even fewer. The government made it clear that whatever loss to the rice producers resulted from the market opening would be amply compensated. But the protection of the rice market became both a symbolic and political issue in a country where rice had been a daily staple for more than a thousand years. It made no difference to detractors that joining the global trading system would be an overwhelming advantage to Korea as a whole.

Coincidentally, when I was serving as ambassador to the United States (2003-2005), the tenth year of Korea's MMA grant for rice was set to expire at the end of 2004. This meant that I was again involved in major negotiations with the United States, one of the largest rice exporting countries, over whether Korea would enact tariffs on its rice or extend the MMA. I personally thought it would be advantageous if we chose the tariffication route like Japan did in 1999, whereby the rice market could be controlled by high import tariffs. However, the government chose the more populist route and we had to negotiate the extension of MMA for another 10 years until 2014. The negotiations dragged on until the last day of 2004.

As a result of the extension of the MMA on rice, Korea had to increase the amount of rice imports by 20,000 tons each year. By 2014, Korea had imported a total of 409,000 tons of rice over twenty years, accounting for nine percent of Korea's total rice production. Eventually, Korea chose to take the tariff route, thereby making another extension of MMA unnecessary.

Those who opposed the rice market opening made several arguments. The first was economic. They contended that because of the high price of rice in the domestic market, importation of less expensive rice from abroad would damage the economic interests of rice producers at home. The second was security. As rice is the staple crop of the Korean people, dependence on foreign producers would threaten the stable supply and price of rice, thereby adversely affecting the food security of Koreans. Third was the political argument, which contended that the rice market opening was the result of collusion between the Korean chaebol and foreign, supranational capital and big powers, such as the United States.

On the other hand, those who supported the opening of the rice market and trade liberalization in general made the following arguments. First, as a country that depends extensively on foreign trade for economic growth, Korea should participate and support the global free trade system. This entails opening the rice market. Second, delaying the tariffication of rice and other agricultural products would only increase the amount of MMA and bring about trade sanctions in other areas. Third, through tariffication, coupled with measures to support the disadvantaged rice producers, Korea could raise the price and quality competitiveness of Korean rice and successfully compete with imported rice.

Thus, opening the market for rice and other agricultural products was both an economic and political issue. In the end, Korea had to adopt the policy of protecting and supporting the producers of rice and other agricultural products while making the Korean products more competitive. With decreasing dependence on rice, it became more feasible and economically viable for Korea to pursue such a two-sided policy on agricultural products.

Back to the University

In Korea in the 1990s, an annual cabinet reshuffle was almost a customary affair. I survived the UR cabinet purging of 1993, and by the end of 1994, I became one of the "long lasting" members of the Kim Young-sam cabinet. Having served as foreign minister for almost two years and put a lid on the North Korean nuclear issue in October with the Geneva Agreed Framework, I was both expecting and hoping to terminate my tenure as foreign minister and return to the university.

At the time, it was also customary for the change of ministers in the cabinet to take place without any prior notice, with the outgoing minister often learning about his or her departure over the radio. My turn to vacate the position came, together with a dozen others, at the end of December.

The day after I learned about my departure (vacating the office, which I had prepared for beforehand, took place on the same day it was announced), President Kim Young-sam asked to see me at the Blue House. As soon as he saw me, the president asked me if I could take up the position of ambassador to the United States, a position that Mr. Han Seung-soo just vacated, as he was called back to become President Kim's chief of staff. I felt that I had already done enough service for the country by serving two strident years as foreign minister. I replied, "I am the only son of my mother, who is over 80 years old. I cannot bring her with me to the United States, and neither can I let her stay in Korea by herself. I hope you will understand that I cannot accept your kind offer this time."

This was indeed a true excuse, but also one often used throughout Korean history to decline the king's order to take up an unwanted position when piety to parents was one of the society's most important virtues. The president was understanding and asked whom I would recommend as the new ambassador to Washington. I suggested Ambassador Park Kun-woo, who was then serving as the vice foreign minister. Ambassador Park was subsequently appointed as Korea's ambassador to the United States and admirably performed his duties.

Three Impressive Diplomats

During the two short years of my tenure as Korean foreign minister, I had the chance to meet many prominent diplomats from countries around the world. I would like to introduce the three most impressive diplomats—Foreign Minister Qian Qichen of China, Foreign Minister Shimon Peres of Israel, and U.N. Secretary-General Boutros Boutros-Ghali of Egypt—and describe some of my interactions with them.

Qian Qichen (1928-2017)

In August 1992, six months before I became foreign minister, Korea and China normalized their diplomatic relations after 43 years of estrangement following the communist takeover of mainland China in 1949. Until China and South Korea began to pursue rapprochement after

Friendly walk with Chinese Foreign Minister Qian Qichen, 1994

the Seoul Olympics in 1988, China, which had intervened in the Korean War on the side of North Korea, was considered one of South Korea's enemies. Thus, when the North Korean nuclear crisis emerged only two weeks after the start of the Kim Young-sam government, I thought it was a stroke of good luck in the midst of misfortune that we had normalized diplomatic relations with China.

As I believed that close cooperation with China was indispensable for the resolution of the North Korean nuclear problem, the opportunity to meet China's Foreign Minister (and concurrently Deputy Prime Minister) Qian Qichen presented itself at the end of March, 1993. Qian and I were to attend the annual meeting of the United Nations Economic and Social Council for Asia and the Pacific (UN ESCAP) in Bangkok, Thailand, and we were to have a bilateral foreign ministers' meeting there. Since I was a new foreign minister and Qian was a veteran diplomat and a dozen years older than me, I could not help but feel somewhat tense before meeting him.

When we met, however, Qian put me at ease immediately with his clear understanding of the issues and warm and friendly attitude. As China's foreign minister, Qian was instrumental during crucial moments of recent Chinese history, including the return of Hong Kong and Macau to Chinese sovereignty and normalizing relations with the West after the Tiananmen Incident in 1989. Regarding the Korean Peninsula, Qian was tasked with visiting Pyongyang in 1992 to inform Kim Il-sung that China would formally establish diplomatic relations with South Korea.[8]

At the Bangkok meeting in March 1993, we came to an understanding that China would allow the North Korean issue at the IAEA to be referred to the U.N. Security Council, while South Korea would consent to a U.S.-North Korea bilateral meeting to discuss the issue. Through this agreement, the path to a bilateral negotiation between the United States and North Korea was opened. From this initial encounter until the end of 1994, I had a total of ten official, bilateral meetings with Qian, often taking advantage of meeting him during multilateral events, such as U.N., ASEAN, or APEC summits.

The most urgent and salient issue in those meetings was North Korea's nuclear weapons program. Each time, China took effective and constructive, if not excessively expressive, measures to bring back to or keep North Korea at the negotiating table and prevent it from taking provocative actions. One prominent example was the handling of the June 1994 crisis.

My cooperative relationship with Mr. Qian was also helpful when we reestablished relations with Taiwan in 1994, which had been severed when relations between South Korea and China were normalized. After extensive negotiations with Taipei and informal consultation with Beijing, we decided to give Taiwan's representative office in Seoul

---

8   Qian Qichen, *Ten Episodes in Chinese Diplomacy*, New York, 2006.

the official-sounding name of "Mission," which probably was a poor but nevertheless important consolatory gesture to Taipei, whose pride was seriously hurt by South Korea's unilateral severance of diplomatic relations.

Minister Qian's wife, Mrs. Zhou Hanqiong, a former diplomat, was an intelligent and amiable lady who got along well with my wife, Yi Song-mi. My wife is well acquainted with Chinese culture and language by virtue of her study of Chinese art. After I left my government post, the Chinese foreign ministry invited both of us to travel around China, including visits to Xian, Lanzhou, and Dunhuang.

Shimon Peres (1923-2016)

Mr. Shimon Peres is best known as the ninth president and two time prime minister of Israel. He also won the 1994 Nobel Peace Prize along with Yitzhak Rabin and Yasser Arafat for the Oslo Accords peace talks. I knew Peres when he was foreign minister, and I found him to be an able strategist and eloquent orator with moderate and pragmatic views in a country where hard-line conservatives often take control. As Israel's president (2007-2014), he had to endure difficult political co-habitation with Prime Minister Benjamin Netanyahu.

Immediately after I assumed the foreign minister's position, I went to work restoring our diplomatic relations with Israel, which had been discontinued in the wake of the "oil shock" in the 1970s. During that time, Seoul was focusing its diplomatic efforts on oil-producing countries in the Middle East. Thus, after Korean-Israeli diplomatic relations were reestablished, I naturally had many opportunities to meet and talk with Mr. Peres.

At the first meeting with Mr. Peres, who was 17 years older than me, I was captivated by his broad knowledge and deep philosophical

With Foreign Minister Shimon Peres of Israel, 1993

insights on international affairs, realistic strategic thinking, and balanced points of view. Every time we met—at the U.N. in New York, in Korea when he and Prime Minister Rabin visited Seoul, in Tel Aviv when I visited Israel as an advisor for the Peres Institute for Peace, I was fortunate to have the opportunity to discuss with him issues related to the Korean Peninsula and the Middle East.

He believed that hard-line responses are necessary only in cases of terrorist attack and unjustified military action, but they could be counterproductive if such tactics are the result of emotional hatred or political necessity. Instead, he reasoned, adversaries would be best off if they sought a win-win solution to their disputes. Indeed, both when he was in the government and out of it, Mr. Peres made great efforts to economically rehabilitate Palestine, and he promoted human rights and sought to secure international, including World Bank, support and aid for such efforts there.

In 1996, he founded the Peres Center for Peace, located in Jaffa, Israel, to foster peace building and economic cooperation between peoples in the Middle East. I was honored to serve as an international member of the Peres Institute, and I visited Israel several times after I left the government in that capacity.

Boutros Boutros-Ghali (1922-2016)

My association with Secretary-General Boutros-Ghali began in 1993 when I assumed the position of foreign minister. I first met him while visiting the United Nations that summer as part of my effort to mobilize international support on the North Korean nuclear crisis. As a former university professor with training in international law and politics, he had much in common with my own background. In the course of my conversation with him, I found him to be a warm-hearted, clear-thinking person and an eloquent speaker. I liked him immediately and developed a high respect for him. He was attentive, understanding, and supportive of our effort to resolve the North Korean issue peacefully and by diplomatic means.

Secretary-General Boutros-Ghali showed much empathy for a divided country such as Korea and was eager to be helpful not only in resolving the nuclear issue, but also in achieving peace, reconciliation, and ultimate reunification of the Korean nation.

In 1994, the Secretary-General took the trouble of visiting both North and South Korea in an effort to reduce tensions on the Peninsula. There was a major obstacle, however. North Korea adamantly refused the Secretary-General's offer to serve as a friendly intermediary between the parties. They insisted that, if negotiation takes place at all, it would be between itself and the United States only. He was disappointed, of course, but he never ceased to be interested, concerned about, and involved in Korean issues, particularly the nuclear one. I found him to be enormously helpful at every step in our effort to find a peaceful

With Boutrus Boutrus-Ghali, UN Secretary-General, 1993

resolution of the problem at hand.

In 1995, after I left the foreign ministry, I was visiting Harvard University to give a series of lectures (known as Reischauer Lectures). I received a telephone call from Boutros-Ghali, who asked me if I would take the responsibility of serving as the Special Representative of the Secretary-General (SRSG) for Cyprus. Cyprus, like Korea, was a divided country; the United Nations had stationed a peace-keeping force (UNFICYP) there since 1964. According to Boutros-Ghali, I would be a good person to deal with the Cyprus problem as I came from another divided country. I recognized that, as the first Asian diplomat dealing with a critical European issue, it would be a formidable challenge for me. But out of respect for the Secretary-General's thoughtful consideration, I accepted the assignment.

From the way that the Secretary-General approached the Cyprus problem, it was clear to me that he had a special affection and concern for small countries, especially divided ones, such as Cyprus and Korea. He did not approve of the bullying or arbitrary actions of big, major powers. During my relatively short term (one and a half years) as the SRSG for Cyprus, we were not able to make any headway towards unifying the country, despite my exhaustive efforts to deal with several factions within Cyprus, as well as other actors, including Turkey, Greece, the European Union, the United States, Great Britain, and the United Nations. The only consolation I had was that I, together with those concerned with peace within Cyprus, was able to prevent a major breakdown of order on the island. Although Boutros-Ghali was to serve only one five-year term until 1996, had he stayed in office longer, I believe that we could have done something to bring the Greek and Turkish Cypriots together and secure the acceptance of their reunification with admission to the European Union.

After Boutros-Ghali finished his term as Secretary-General, he returned to the private sector and concentrated his efforts on two important fronts: progress in the developing world through the South Center, which he chaired, and promotion of democracy and human rights on the global level. On the latter issue, he chaired the UNESCO project for "democracy and human rights in the Middle East." I was honored to be invited to two conferences convened in Byblos, Lebanon, and Cairo, Egypt for this important, yet very difficult, project.

I had an extraordinary experience and witnessed the true quality of Boutros-Ghali when I attended the Cairo meeting on democracy in the Middle East in 2005. That year, a presidential election in Egypt was scheduled and President Mubarak was facing nine other candidates. Unfortunately, however, the Al-Ghad (Tomorrow) Party's Ayman Nur, an outspoken critic of Mubarak, was jailed and facing trial. When the international participants of the conference returned to the conference room after a luncheon break, we found that many of our seats had been taken over and occupied by protesters (including Ayman Nur's wife) who were demanding the freedom of the jailed candidate and a free presidential election. What ensued was a shouting match between the protesters and some Egyptian participants. The protesters apparently argued (we learned through partial interpretation of our Arabic-speaking fellow participants) that there was no use in having a conference on democracy and human rights when their candidate was being jailed on trumped-up, political charges. The Egyptian conference participants argued that the protesters had no right to disrupt an international meeting which was being held to promote democracy and human rights in the Middle East. What restored order to the crowd and ensured the orderly exit of the protesters was Boutros-Ghali's calm and assuring statement that it was precisely the purpose of the conference to bring about democratic, fair, and free elections in Egypt and around the Middle East. I felt then that Boutros-Ghali was a man of conviction and persuasive skill.

Chapter 4

Ambassador in Washington

The Beginning

When President (2003-2008) Roh Moo-hyun, offered me the position of ambassador to the United States, I was neither excited about nor willing to take him up on the offer. To begin with, I did not quite like the idea of a former high-level official in the government assuming the post of ambassador in Washington, a position that all able career diplomats in the foreign ministry aspired to take. Secondly, I knew that regardless of who was appointed, the tenure as South Korea's ambassador to the U.S. in 2003 was not exactly going to be a picnic. One would be caught between the hard-line policies of the U.S. and the soft-line policies of South Korea, vis-à-vis North Korea. This would be the exact opposite of my position when I was foreign minister. At that time, I was caught between a hard-line South Korean president and a more accommodating U.S. administration. Nevertheless, out of a sense of responsibility to save the U.S.-Korea alliance and serve the country, I agreed to accept the challenge.

I knew what I was getting into when I accepted the offer to become ambassador to the U.S. in March 2003. At the time, many Koreans who wanted to maintain good relations with the U.S. were concerned that U.S.-ROK relations were off to a rocky start with the election of President Roh. It was no secret that Roh had been elected partly on the strength of anti-U.S. demonstrations precipitated by the death of two middle-school girls in a traffic accident caused by two U.S. soldiers on a training mission. In fact, Roh's supporters took advantage of the accident by galvanizing anti-U.S. sentiment to the fullest extent, with candlelight vigils, rallies, and demonstrations denouncing the U.S. and the U.S. troop presence in Korea. Unlike his predecessors, Roh, who was only four years old at the time of the Korean War, had no personal memory of the conflict and no deep feelings of gratitude toward the United States for having come to the aid of South Korea after the communist invasion. He once famously asked the question, "What's wrong with being anti-American?"

With President Roh at the day of my appointment as Ambassador to the U.S. April 19, 2003

So I had my work cut out for me as ambassador to Washington. Among the many tasks I had before me, two stood out. One was to assure the Bush administration that President Roh was not anti-American after all and that his intention was to have good relations with the United States. The second was to make sure that the U.S. did not overreact to the North Korean nuclear program or seek to attack North Korea and precipitate an armed conflict on the Korean Peninsula. But my immediate task after arriving in Washington was to prepare for President Roh's scheduled visit to Washington in May. Howard French of the *New York Times* wrote an article about my challenge with the title, "Korean Diplomacy Enters a New Era" on April 20, 2003, the day of my arrival in the U.S.[9] Here is what French wrote in the article.

"Next month, a new South Korean president, Roh Moo Hyun, will travel to Washington.

He will be preceded, though, by a new ambassador, Han Sung Joo. Experts on South Korea both here and in the United States say the choice of Mr. Han reflects a determination to avoid a diplomatic train wreck.

In Mr. Han, the experts say, Mr. Roh has chosen someone who can take the initiative on complicated and sensitive diplomacy rather than merely to try to burnish his leader's image. This former foreign minister and university president has ideas of his own, and in his confident, though soft-spoken way, he does not hesitate to voice them."

Difference between a Minister and an Ambassador

The first thing I found after arriving in Washington was that there was considerable difference between being a foreign minister and serving as an ambassador. In essence, minister is a policy *making*

---

9 French, Howard. "Korean Diplomacy Enters a New Era." *The New York Times*, April 20, 2003, p. 5.

position and ambassador is a policy *implementing* position. Furthermore, I found that under the Roh Moo-hyun government, the foreign ministry itself became something of a secondary agency in foreign policymaking relative to the Blue House, including policy related to the North Korean nuclear issue, which reemerged as a crisis situation. For these reasons, I could not help but feel that my role in policymaking was far smaller as ambassador than when I was the minister.

Overall, the assistants and advisors in the Blue House were persons who could be classified as "progressives" or people on the left, in that they placed more emphasis on *jaju*, or national assertiveness, relative to the alliance with the U.S. Their views tended to prevail over the more alliance-oriented approaches pursued by the foreign ministry and defense ministry.

As ambassador in Washington, I could play a role in swaying the president toward a more pragmatic and alliance-oriented approach in contrast to what his left-leaning *aides de camp* would suggest. I would advise him that, in order to persuade the U.S. to take a more moderate stance toward North Korea, it was important to help them in areas in which it needed Korea's cooperation, such as the war effort in Iraq. At the same time, I would explain to my American interlocutors that President Roh, because he was a "progressive" president whose political base consisted of those strongly opposed to "pro-American" measures, could actually get away with doing more for the U.S., such as dispatching Korean troops to Iraq. In other words, because of his less-than-friendly *words* toward the United States, he could politically afford to initiate friendly actions regarding the United States.

Credential Presentation

My *agrément* as ambassador was granted by the United States in an almost record time of nine days after the Korean government requested it. I arrived in the United States on April 20th and was able to present my credentials to President Bush in time for the summit meeting in May.

In most other countries, when the ambassador's credentials are presented, he or she is accompanied by one or two members of the embassy staff. In the case of the United States, only the ambassador's family members are allowed to participate. I was accompanied by several members of my family, including my wife (Song-mi), son (Charles Sungwon), daughter-in-law (Susan Kobayashi), grand-daughter (Mina), grand-son (Dylan), and a couple of Song-mi's nephews (Kim Hanhoe and family and Kim Jong-ju) who happened to be studying or visiting in the United States.

As I was the last one that afternoon to present credentials in a group

President Bush and the Han family on the occasion of presentation of the ambassador's credential, 2003

of four ambassadors, President Bush spent considerable time talking not only with me, but also with my family. I found the president friendly, focused on the issues when necessary, unpretentious, and even humorous with the family and children.

My wife Song-mi had come to Washington the previous day to attend the credentials presentation after visiting Houston, Texas, where she gave a lecture on her specialty, Korean art. When President Bush heard about her professional activity in Houston he was very interested, as Texas is his home state and Houston, his base city. He looked at me and remarked in jest, "So, you married up like me." Since I had never heard that expression before, I had to look it up afterwards in the English-Korean dictionary I carried all the time.

Of course, President Bush did not forget to ask me to convey his warmest regards to President Roh and to promise a successful summit meeting with him, scheduled for a couple of weeks later.

The First Summit

I was fully aware that my mission would not be easy. President Bush had just labeled North Korea a member of the "axis of evil." President Roh was openly critical of the "unequal" Korea-U.S. relationship. However, I also had an inkling that the meeting could turn out well. For one thing, I knew both presidents wished to avoid the disaster of two years earlier and to make their first meeting a successful one.

In fact, one month before President Roh's scheduled visit to Washington, President Bush's father, former president George H. W. Bush, traveled to Seoul to size up Mr. Roh and to let him know what his son was like. The senior Bush assured the Korean president that the two of them would surely hit it off, as they were quite alike: straightforward,

50th Anniversary Memorial for the Korean War deaths, 2003

spontaneous, unpretentious, and personable. "I know my son," the elder Bush said, "just tell him like it is. President Bush will like it, and you two will get along fine." The former U.S. president was very encouraging.

When the two presidents actually met, those who were present could see that they were both trying hard to be agreeable to each other. President Roh acknowledged and expressed gratitude for the U.S. contribution to Korea's security. He did not dispute President Bush's rather unkind characterization of the North Korean regime. President Bush reiterated the firm U.S. commitment to peace, security, and denuclearization of the Korean Peninsula. President Bush's interactions with Roh seemed genuine, as he later described Roh as an "easy man to talk with," even though that description was taken by Roh's critics at home (many of whom were members of his own party) as proof that President Roh was buckling under the pressure of the United States.

In due course, however, the bilateral relationship improved and recovered its solvency. South Korea sent troops to Iraq, becoming the third-largest contingent after the United States and the United Kingdom. The two governments agreed on the relocation of U.S. troops in Korea, and South Korea accepted the principle of strategic flexibility (this "flexibility" meaning the United States sought to deploy U.S. troops stationed in Korea to other areas if necessary) with regard to USFK. They also agreed on the transfer of wartime operational control of the Korean armed forces by the year 2012. Before the end of his presidential term, President Roh would even succeed in negotiating a free trade agreement with the United States.

In fact, the Roh Moo-hyun administration was staffed with individuals (sometimes referred to as "the Taliban" in Washington) who focused on creating a more independent and balanced relationship with the United States. Yet, overall, it was judged by the Bush administration to be "better in deeds than in words" in conducting its relationship with the United States. In fact, the Roh government was better able to persuade the National Assembly to accept the government's decision to dispatch troops to Iraq precisely because it was Roh's own political supporters who put up the fiercest opposition.

Troop Dispatch to Iraq

The top priority for President Bush, while I was serving in Washington, was conducting the war in Iraq. Earlier, in October 2001, when the U.S. invaded Afghanistan in the wake of the 9/11 attacks, the military operation was approved by the U.N. Security Council and supported by NATO (North Atlantic Treaty Organization).

However, when the U.S. invaded Iraq in March 2003 with the ostensible purpose of punishing Saddam Hussein for his support of terrorism and development of weapons of mass destruction, many countries, including America's allies, did not go along. Normally friendly countries, such as France and Germany and neighbors Canada and Mexico, did not approve of the 2003 U.S. invasion of Iraq.

The U.S. nevertheless conducted the warfare in lightning fast fashion, described as a "shock and awe" blitzkrieg. Victory was declared 40 days after combat began. On May 1, President George W. Bush, a former pilot in the Air National Guard Reserve, co-piloted an airplane to the U.S. aircraft carrier *Abraham Lincoln* where a banner proclaiming "Mission Accomplished" was prominently hung and a victory ceremony was held. However, the war did not, in fact, end. Fierce resistance persisted, particularly among Sunnis (Saddam Hussein's base) displaced by Shiites, and American soldier casualties began to mount.

The "Iraq War," as it was being called in the United States, was understood as a war of choice rather than one of necessity, and it became increasingly unpopular. Nevertheless, the administration decided that it needed to increase the number of combat troops. Eventually, it asked some of its allies and other countries to dispatch troops to supplement the U.S. forces. As a result, a total of 22,000 soldiers from 31 countries, including Britain and Korea, were dispatched to Iraq to assist the U.S. war efforts.

In sending the troop dispatch request to the National Assembly for approval, President Roh stated that it had to be done for the sake of the alliance with the United States, even though he was not in full agreement with the rationale for the war. Although the remark did not go over well in Washington, the U.S. government had no choice but to accept it as necessary rhetoric for what was a very controversial decision in Korea.

I had a chance to talk, one on one, about the issue with President Roh when I visited Seoul in October of 2003 before accompanying him to the Bangkok APEC (Asia-Pacific Economic Cooperation) summit

Conferring a Korean medal of honor to Admiral Robert F. Willard, 2004

meeting. I explained that it would be in our interest to dispatch Korean troops to Iraq, as the U.S. had sent troops to Korea during the Korean War and subsequently suffered many casualties (nearly 37,000 killed). I also stressed that it would strengthen the U.S.-Korea alliance and boost our position vis-à-vis the U.S. when we conferred on our approach toward North Korea. I also emphasized the importance of minimizing our potential casualties if and when our troops were sent to Iraq.

President Roh was persuaded by my argument, if he had not been persuaded already, and decided to dispatch Korean troops to Iraq. Eventually a total of 3,000 troops were sent to Irvil, a Kurdistan region in Northern Iraq. They were referred to as the *Zaytun* (meaning olive in Arabic and symbolizing peace) regiment. Although the troops were supposed to be engaged in non-combative activities, combat troops for self-protection were included.

During a period of 4 years and 3 months, a total of 19,000 Korean troops were deployed in Iraq for maintaining domestic peace and security, medical service, technical education, and construction of public infrastructure before their complete withdrawal in December 2007. Among the troops dispatched to Iraq, one Korean soldier was killed by an improvised explosive device (IED).

The saddest event during my stay in Washington took place in June 2004, when a Korean civilian military supply contractor, Kim Sun-il was kidnapped and killed by a militant jihadist group called Jama'at al-Tawhid wal-Jihad. Three weeks before he was killed, Kim was kidnapped by the group, which was led by the internationally known terrorist, Abu Musab al Zarqawi. After his kidnapping was reported by the Arabic broadcasting network al Jazeera, the Korean government made every possible diplomatic effort for his release, but to no avail.

This was the first incident of a Korean kidnapped and killed by a terrorist organization. As the Korean ambassador in Washington, all I could do was to try to obtain information and intelligence from the U.S. government and seek their support for the victim's release. After his death, which became the subject of much media attention both in Korea and abroad, Korean diplomatic efforts, including those of the embassy in Washington, were criticized for their inability to save him. Since the kidnappers demanded the withdrawal of Korean troops from Iraq as a quid pro quo for Kim's release, the government was further criticized for refusing to accept the kidnappers' ultimatums. The government decided, however, that, despite the tragic circumstances, the kidnapper's demands (or the demands of any kidnapper in fact) could not be the basis for the government's actions, as it would only encourage more kidnappings.

The North Korea Conundrum

Despite cooperation on troop dispatches to the Iraq War,

Washington and Seoul remained at odds over the question of how to deal with North Korea until the Roh administration's final year. The Bush administration remained firm on its hard-line stance toward North Korea and the nuclear issue. Initially, the Bush team was critical of the Clinton administration's 1994 Geneva Agreed Framework. President Bush opposed bilateral talks with one of what he called "axis of evil" countries. And the administration was also against "rewarding" North Korea for its bad behavior. It insisted on a 2003 Libya-style solution to the North Korean nuclear problem.

By contrast, President Roh Moo-hyun's view was that North Korea had developed its nuclear program because of a keen sense of insecurity in the face of the overwhelming military might of the United States and prosperous South Korea. Roh's argument was: "If the source of insecurity is removed, North Korea will rid itself of nuclear weapons and the nuclear weapons program." This was what he insisted both in private and in public. The Bush administration found it hard to understand what it considered a "naïve" view of the North Korean nuclear threat. From the other side, the Roh administration could neither accept nor understand President Bush's inflexible hard-line policy toward the North. These two diametrically opposite perspectives brought about friction and wrangling not only in bilateral consultations, but also in multilateral settings such as the Japan-South Korea-U.S. Trilateral Coordination and Oversight Group (known as TCOG) meetings and the Six-Party Talks. Worse yet, it resulted in the erosion of trust and friendship between the two longtime allies.

But in a series of events that culminated on February 13, 2007, the United States made an about-face. It decided to negotiate with North Korea on a bilateral basis and to reward North Korea for its "good behavior," that is, for freezing, declaring, and dismantling its nuclear weapons, materials, and facilities. But, even without complete dismantlement of the program and a full declaration of all nuclear-related activities, the Bush administration became willing to provide certain rewards, including removing North Korea from the list of state sponsors of terrorism, lifting restrictions on North Korean trade under the Trading with the Enemy Act, and providing energy, food, and security assurances.

The South Korean government, which had been advocating engagement with North Korea, welcomed the policy change. Its reasoning was that engagement, rather than pressure, would lessen the sense of insecurity felt by the North Korean regime and would bring about a change of heart, policy, and society. Before this convergence of views, however, the task fell upon South Korea's ambassador to Washington to maintain clear lines of communication, sustain trust and friendship, and prevent differences from escalating into misunderstanding and suspicion between the two countries. One critical occasion came in December 2004, when President Roh made a stopover in Los Angeles on his way to Santiago, Chile, for an Asia-Pacific Economic Cooperation (APEC) summit. Speaking to a World Affairs Council audience, he made several points to the consternation of his aides, who had tried in vain to dissuade him. Roh stated that he could understand why North Korea would wish to have nuclear weapons, that it was a sense of insecurity which led North Korea down the nuclear path, and that he was convinced that once the sense of insecurity was removed, North Korea would denuclearize itself.

Whatever the motivation or reasoning behind his remarks, one thing was certain: It was sure to cause raised eyebrows and disappointment, if not outright anger, in Washington. After the speech, I told President Roh that I would come to Santiago to be present at the scheduled bilateral summit with President Bush on the sidelines of the APEC summit. Since President Roh was planning to spend a few days visiting other South

American countries before proceeding to Chile, I had time to talk with the White House officials. In my meeting, I explained that President Roh had profound and genuine concerns about the possibility of military conflict breaking out on the Korean Peninsula, and his wish was that the North Korean nuclear issue would be resolved in a peaceful and mutually beneficial way.

I have no way of knowing how effective my explanation was. However, we agreed that it would be best for relations between our two countries and for our ability to deal with North Korea if President Roh's Los Angeles remarks did not become an issue at the forthcoming Santiago summit. As it happened, President Bush, who surely must have been briefed about them, did not even mention the remarks at the meeting, much less question their meaning or purpose. But, to everyone's surprise, President Roh did. He did so to explain that his remarks were intended to rebuke, not the policy of the Bush administration, but the views expressed by some "very hard-line" commentators in Washington, D.C. To his credit, and to the relief of others present, President Bush chose not to prolong that part of the summit discussion.

Politics and Diplomacy

In addition to dealing with the enormous difference in perspective between South Korea and the United States regarding North Korea, I also had to deal with politics back home and in Washington. Politics in Korea were such that predictable and orderly diplomacy was impossible. In March 2004, 11 months after my arrival in Washington, President Roh was impeached by the National Assembly, although the impeachment was eventually overturned by the Constitutional Court. That left a gap of some two months, during which there was no presidential leadership coming from Seoul. This respite actually seemed to be a mixed blessing for Korea's diplomacy in the United States. For the most part, however, during the 22 months of my Washington assignment, I had to operate in a situation where the Foreign Ministry was greatly marginalized in the face of a meddlesome Blue House. This was an unfamiliar situation for me, as when I had served earlier as the foreign minister, the ministry was the center for creating policy initiatives and following through with implementation strategies.

The situation was not much better in Washington, where the State Department, headed by Colin Powell, seemed to have a number of policy differences with the vice president's office and sometimes with the Defense Department, led by Donald Rumsfeld. Policy schisms seemed to be present even within the State Department, where the nonproliferation bureau run by Under Secretary of State John Bolton stuck to its hard-line stance toward North Korea. In such an environment, in which there were policy differences within both the home and host governments, it was difficult for a Korean ambassador to advocate any policy without offending one faction or another in each of the two governments. Therefore, it was important for me to steer clear of the ideological fights between factions or departments, to frame positions and formulas as rationally and pragmatically as possible, and to encourage the respective agencies within each of the two governments to work together.

The same was true in dealing with both houses of the U.S. Congress. The Korea-related issues in which members of Congress were particularly interested boiled down to trade with South Korea and human rights in North Korea. On trade, legislators from beef and automobile-producing states were understandably insistent on market liberalization and "level trading" with South Korea. In addition to playing the messenger role of conveying complaints, requests, and appeals to the home government, the ambassador also had to put out the fires in cases of trade litigation and imposition of penalties.

On the issue of human rights in North Korea, even if the ambassador fully shared the concerns of the U.S. members of Congress on the subject, I had to explain the practicality and limits of raising the issue. There was the need to balance promoting North Korean human rights openly and rigorously with the need to be effective on multiple issues, such as the nuclear problem. North Korea regarded the call for enforcing human rights as a call for the demise of the regime itself. Therefore, the regime would be far more sensitive and resistant when they are the focus of human rights campaigns, as compared with either the former Soviet Union or China, which were, and are, far less vulnerable to outside calls for human rights.

At any given time, Washington is home to around 150 ambassadors from abroad who are serving for a variety of reasons: they may be the most able (and possibly most senior) diplomats of their country, a politically influential person, a close associate or friend of the country's leadership, an intellectually able and respected person, or some combination of these traits. Washington's diplomatic community is not the kind of closely knit group usually found in other countries because of its large size, the diverse backgrounds of its members, and their busy schedules. Still, I was able to establish good personal rapport with many ambassadors, particularly those from Asia and Europe. I received excellent assistance from Ambassador Chan Heng Chee of Singapore, whom I had known for many years in the Asian academic circuit and who had already been in Washington as ambassador for four years by the time I arrived. She introduced me not only to ambassadors from other countries but also to leading members of the media, nongovernmental organizations, the business sector, Congress, and the administration.

I had good and close relationships with the Association of Southeast Asian Nations (ASEAN) ambassadors, as well as the Chinese and

Japanese ambassadors, whom I met regularly to discuss matters related to our common concerns. My affinity with the European ambassadors was partly attributable to the fact that I had worked with some of them when I was serving as the U.N. Secretary-General's special representative for Cyprus. That experience also gave me the opportunity to establish a good relationship with ambassadors from Turkey, Greece, and Cyprus. It was a coincidence that I presented my credentials to President Bush on the same day as the ambassador from Rwanda, a country I had worked on as a member of the U.N. Commission of Inquiry (COI) for the 1994 genocide. On every subsequent diplomatic occasion, the Rwandan ambassador, a young man with a newborn baby, and I were standing or sitting side by side, as ambassadors are customarily placed in the same order as the presentation of our credentials.

It was fortuitous that I was able to witness firsthand the 2004 presidential election during my term as ambassador. I observed the Democratic and Republican National Conventions in Boston and New York, respectively, which were a spectacle to watch if not very inspirational. The only phrase that I remember from either convention is not from one of the nominees, John Kerry or George W. Bush, but from Ted Sorenson (who had served as speechwriter for President John F. Kennedy). After being helped to the podium of the Democratic Party convention, Sorenson said, "I am losing my eyesight, but I still have my vision." The only debate on Korea between the candidates during the campaign was whether the United States should negotiate with North Korea bilaterally or only on a six-party basis. President Bush was emphatic that he would not allow bilateral talks with North Korea, though in fact he did two years later. President Bush was reelected for another four-year term despite his administration's Iraq venture. In his second inauguration speech on January 20, 2005, President Bush emphasized the need and importance of spreading democracy and human

Mr. Hwang Jang-yop, the defector, visits Washington, D.C., 2004

rights throughout the world. The ambassadors, together with members of the U.S. Congress and other government officials, were treated to the Wilsonian phrase, "Spreading democracy will bring peace."

In an article entitled, "South Korean Ambassador Knows How to Keep His Cool," Nora Boustany of the *Washington Post* wrote as follows about me.[10]

> *"The serenity of the South Korean ambassador, Han Sung Joo, is almost unnerving. But ultimately, his composure and calm in the face of the many storms he has weathered since arriving in Washington last year come off as admirable and inspiring."*
>
> *"Han, who runs an embassy staff of 150, learned his motto in life from his mother: "Be gentle to a gentle person and tough to a tough person. Be firm with superiors and kind to subordinates."*
>
> *"A decision by South Korea's parliament to dispatch an additional 3,000 troops was intensely debated. But "we had this ironic advantage, Han said. Most of the opponents to sending more troops were the ones who had*

---

10   http://www.washingtonpost.com/wp-dyn/articles/A53683-2004Jul15.html.

voted for the president's party."

"It took Han and his wife, an art historian, some time to warm to the huge and impersonal ambassador's residence, and his responsibilities have been huge. But he is grateful for the opportunity to put his abilities to good use.

It's all part of the deal, he said, smiling. Like all seasoned survivors, he has learned to be outwardly soft and inwardly strong, just as his mother taught him."

The Departure from Washington, D.C.

In early February 2005, I was preparing to leave Washington for home after 22 months as Korea's ambassador to the United States. My final official act as ambassador would be to bid farewell to Condoleezza Rice, the Secretary of State, who had assumed office in the second George W. Bush administration only a couple of weeks before. I had not had the chance to meet her earlier because she had embarked on an official nine-country visit to Europe and the Middle East shortly after assuming office on January 26, 2005.

Then the opportunity came. My visit to the State Department was initially set in order to fulfill three specific objectives: to accompany South Korea's foreign minister on his visit to meet the new secretary of state, to discuss North Korea's recent official declaration that it possessed nuclear weapons, and to bid my official adieu to the secretary.

As expected, the meeting was dominated by topic number two: how to respond to the official declaration, made only a few days before, that North Korea possessed nuclear weapons. Predictably, South Korea's foreign minister emphasized that there was no need to take the North's claim at face value. North Korea was most likely bluffing in order to

Between Colin Powell and Condoleeza Rice, 2003

attract U.S. attention and lure the U.S. to the bilateral negotiating table. In any case, the foreign minister argued that we (meaning mainly the U.S.) should not overreact. This was a position South Korea had taken consistently since the second nuclear crisis erupted in October 2002: North Korean nuclear weapons were not much of a threat to the rest of the world, and therefore the U.S. should not overreact. In fact, since President Roh assumed office in February 2003, his main concern was not that North Korea would achieve nuclear weapons capability. Rather, he was more concerned that the U.S. would attack North Korea using a surgical strike and precipitate a military conflict on the Korean Peninsula.

For once, Secretary Rice agreed that we (meaning both the United States and the Republic of Korea) should downplay the tense situation. In other words, we should not be pushed into playing the North Korean game of "ratcheting it up and making us panic." It was understandable that the United States, including Rice herself, did not want to make the North's declaration a big issue, as they had already been focusing on the North Korean nuclear issue for some time. In particular, the administration had confronted the North over its covert uranium enrichment in October 2002.

When the North refused to acknowledge its uranium enrichment program, the U.S. suspended its monthly supply of heavy fuel oil, as stipulated in the October 1994 Geneva Agreed Framework. In response, the North Koreans resumed their nuclear program and the operation of a five-megawatt nuclear reactor, which was used for producing plutonium through the reprocessing of spent fuel. Since then, the U.S. had pressed for the North to come clean on the issue, insisting on CVID, meaning the "complete, verifiable, and irreversible dismantlement" of the North's nuclear weapons program. The U.S. was seeking CVID regardless of whether the nuclear program was based on plutonium or the enrichment of uranium.

The apparent toughness of the U.S. policy masked the fact that they had tied their own hands regarding successive violations by North Korea on the nuclear issue. The U.S. was neither able to negotiate with North Korea nor follow through with a hard-line policy when Pyongyang crossed an imaginary red line, such as reactivating the Yongbyon nuclear reactor, reprocessing the spent nuclear fuel, or even declaring that the regime had nuclear weapons. In fact, the U.S. refrained from drawing or specifying any red line at all. The reason I heard for this refusal (indeed inability) to specify a red line or to set a time frame for CVID was because the policymakers were sure that, if a specific red line were drawn, then North Korea would eventually cross it. The same applied with any time frame. If North Korea were to cross this line, the U.S. would not be able to do anything about the situation and would be exposed as a paper tiger. Bogged down in Iraq since 2003 and urged by allies, such as South Korea, and "friends" like China not to undertake any rash actions, the U.S. had no viable options for dealing with the

North, and North Korea itself was intent upon taking advantage of this predicament.

So it happened that the interests of the U.S. and South Korea converged at the time of my farewell call on Secretary Rice. The U.S. did not want to admit that its hard-line policy had failed to prevent North Korea from becoming a country with nuclear weapons. Neither did they want to promise something that they could not deliver, such as absolute zero tolerance of North Korea possessing nuclear weapons. The South Korean government was only too happy to find the U.S. sanguine and relaxed because, despite how provocative and dangerous the North Korean declaration may have sounded, South Korea did not wish to see the international community, in particular the United States, overreacting to the declaration.

Yet, under the circumstances, the two governments could not be perceived as doing nothing. The best solution that both sides could come up with was a series of visible, high-level meetings, such as the one between the U.S. secretary of state and South Korea's foreign minister occurring that day. In fact, they planned a full schedule of meetings that would occur between government officials involved in the six-party talks, including officials from Japan, China, Russia, the United States, and South Korea—but excluding North Korea. "You mean we conduct 'calendar diplomacy'?" Secretary Rice inquired with a smile when the South Korean foreign minister suggested the schedules for such meetings.

Having previously served as South Korea's foreign minister, I could barely contain my frustration with the way this high-level meeting was being conducted. I felt that coming to some kind of positive consensus on how to approach North Korea and how to deal with its official declaration on nuclear weapons possession was critical. When I had meetings with my U.S. counterparts as foreign minister, we would not have bothered figuring out such details as when and where to set up future meetings. Instead, our meeting would have been more like a brainstorming session to devise a real and substantive response. We would have discussed what the consequences would be of doing nothing, how the two countries could approach the situation together, and what kind of response we could give that would be both meaningful and effective.

However, this time around, there was very little cooperative brainstorming on how to deal with North Korea or its nuclear issue. This was due either to the fact that the two countries had grown so far apart in their respective ways of thinking that they had very few options to pursue or because the two sides were unable to work together as a result of their extremely different temperaments, ideologies, and backgrounds. In fact, meetings between the two sides at every level tended to resemble a negotiation between adversaries or an attempt to create a façade of harmony where little existed. Ironically, only when the North Koreans declared that they possessed nuclear weapons did the two sides come together to choose a coordinated response (such as it was) without the need for a public relations campaign. Yet this choice to coordinate approaches was made by both countries for very different reasons.

The meeting was not a complete loss, though, when it came to my ego. It was held at a time when the U.S. ambassador to Korea of three years, Thomas Hubbard, had just left Seoul, and the Bush administration had not nominated his successor. The South Korean government was eager to see a high-profile individual appointed to succeed Ambassador Hubbard. Minister Ban Ki-moon duly urged Secretary Rice to find a good replacement immediately. Secretary Rice, who knew that I was about to leave my post in Washington, turned to me and said with a smile, "Are you interested?" Lest my fellow Koreans misunderstand this remark made in jest, I should emphasize that she was only joking. It was also a joke when I replied, "Some people in Korea already say that I act more like an American ambassador."

Return to Seoul

I returned to Seoul in February 2005. As an ambassador's term goes, 22 months is somewhat short. There were two reasons why, in the summer of 2004, I wrote to President Roh and told him that I wanted to leave the post of ambassador to Washington. One was that I thought my main reason for coming to Washington—to prevent the proverbial "diplomatic train wreck"—had been accomplished. The second was that my retirement from the Korean university where I was a professor was coming up in the spring of 2006. As I had taken a leave of absence from the university, I wanted to go back and have at least one more year of regular teaching before my retirement. I was grateful that President Roh granted my wish, and I was happy to be going back home.

Still, I felt something was missing. It was not like leaving the office of the foreign minister back in December 1994 after another 22 months of service. At the time, I felt a sense of satisfaction that we had put a lid on the North Korean nuclear issue. When I left the Foreign Ministry, ROK-U.S. relations was in relatively good condition. This time, 10 years later, I left the ambassadorial post with the North Korean nuclear issue unresolved and bilateral relations in an uncertain state, with the trust and friendship between the two countries yet to be fully recovered. When I left Washington in 2005, I could only hope that sometime in the near future the holding pattern on both of these fronts would make progress. Now, as of mid-2018, still holding on to that hope, I strive to do what I can outside of the government.

Chapter 5

A Civilian Diplomat
in a Multilateral World

During the ten-year period (1994-2003) between my tenure as South Korea's foreign minister and ambassador to the United States, I was involved in several diplomatic activities as a civilian, but in the context of inter-governmental diplomacy. There were three that stood out, two in connection with the United Nations and one related to East Asian regional cooperation. I served as the Special Representative of the UN Secretary-General (SRSG) for Cyprus (1996-1997), a member of the United Nations Commission of Inquiry for the Rwanda Genocide (April-December, 1997), and chairman of the East Asian Vision Group (1998-2000). In this chapter, I will describe those activities and their results.[11]

Cyprus: Special Representative of the Secretary-General of the United Nations

In the spring of 1996, I was spending three months at Harvard

---

11 United Nations, Report of the independent inquiry into the actions of the United Nations during the 1994 genocide in Rwanda, 15 Dec 1999.

Cyprus patrol, 1996

University as a fellow of the Fairbank Center for Asian Studies at the invitation of Professor Ezra Vogel, a close friend and colleague of mine, who was then serving as the director of the center. I received a telephone call from the U.N. Secretary-General Boutros Boutros-Ghali, who asked me to succeed former Prime Minister of Canada Joe Clark as the Secretary-General's Special Representative for Cyprus, as he was soon scheduled to leave the position.

Secretary-General Boutros-Ghali's choice of me as his special representative for Cyprus was probably due to the fact that I recently served as the foreign minister of Korea, which is, like Cyprus, a divided country. Thus began my venture into European affairs on behalf of the United Nations, which very few Asians had done in earnest. In fact, I was one of the first high-level Asians (Assistant Secretary-General level) to deal with European affairs. The only exception was Yasushi Akashi of Japan, who had served as the head of the U.N. peacekeeping mission for the former Yugoslavia in 1993.

Cyprus was divided when Turkish troops occupied more than a third of the island following the 1974 Greek Cypriot military coup d'état, which threatened the lives of Turkish Cypriots. Following these events, the United Nations Security Council (UNSC) extended and expanded the mission to prevent the dispute from turning into full-scale war. The United Nations Peacekeeping Force in Cyprus (UNFICYP) was redeployed to patrol the United Nations Buffer Zone in Cyprus and assist in the maintenance of the military status quo. Since its establishment, the force has also worked in concert with the Special Representative of the Secretary-General (SRSG) and representatives of the two communities (Greek and Turkish) to seek an amicable diplomatic solution to the problem.

As Dr. Boutros-Ghali explained to me, my responsibilities as the Special Representative of the Secretary-General were: 1) to resolve conflicts; 2) to promote reconciliation, cooperation and integration between the two sides; 3) to communicate with and between the two leaderships; 4) to consult with other concerned governments and secure their cooperation; 5) to facilitate communication and understanding with the headquarters in New York; and 6) to inspect, support and encourage the troops in UNFICYP. In 1996, when I visited Cyprus for the first time, the commander of the U.N. Peacekeeping force in Cyprus was an Argentinean general. Argentina had also contributed a helicopter to patrol the "Green Line" that separated Greek and Turkish Cyprus. A few years later, a Korean general (General Hwang Jin-ha, a former military attaché to Washington D.C. who later became a member of the South Korean National Assembly) served as the UNFICYP commander.

Upon receiving the assignment, I thought it was necessary to look into the history and current situation in Cyprus. Cyprus is located very close to Turkey, so that one can see on a clear day the southern shore of Turkish Anatolia, and to Syria, Lebanon, and Israel to the west (about a 30-minute flight from Cyprus). As a result of its geography, Cyprus had been subjected to numerous invasions and occupation by Mycenae, Egypt, Persia, Macedonia of Alexander the Great, Rome, the Byzantine Empire, the Ottoman Empire, Turkey, and most recently Great Britain, which made Cyprus a Crown colony. Although Cyprus gained independence in 1960 as a result of an agreement made by Britain, Greece, and Turkey. Britain still maintains what are known as "sovereign bases" in Acrotiri and Dekelia, which serve as important air bases for Britain and the United States. As a whole, Northern (Turkish) and Southern (Greek) Cyprus have a population of about 800,000, 78% of whom are predominantly Orthodox Christian Greek Cypriots. Turkish Cypriots, mostly Muslems, comprise about 18%, with the rest being various Christian denominations.

On July 15, 1974, the Greek military junta under Dimitrios Ioannides carried out a coup d'état in Cyprus to unite the island with Greece. In response to the coup, the Turkish army invaded the island. International pressure led to a ceasefire, but by then 36% of the island had been taken over by the Turks and 180,000 Greek Cypriots had been evicted from their homes in the north. At the same time, around 50,000 Turkish Cypriots moved to the areas under the control of the Turkish Forces and settled in the properties of the displaced Greek Cypriots.

In order to understand Cyprus better before going there, I read a book recommended by a regional expert, entitled *Bitter Lemons* by Lawrence Durrell (first published in 1957). Durrell was in Cyprus in the 1930s as a British bureaucrat and wrote about the life and characteristics of Greek and Turkish Cypriots as he saw them. According to Durrell, Greeks and Turks lived together in Cyprus for hundreds of years and developed a complex sense of disdain and acceptance. He observed that Greeks tended to change moods quickly and be quite expressive (like Koreans?), while the Turks were less volatile, but once provoked,

could be rather ferocious. My own
experience 60 years later seemed to
verify what Durrell had observed.
Durrell's old house, "The Bitter
Lemons House," is still standing
and is visited by tourists on the
hills of Bellapais, on the Turkish
(northern) side of the presently
divided Cyprus.

Each time I visited Cyprus
for my assignment, it took at least
more than two weeks of travel
time. In order to go to Nicosia (the
capital of Cyprus) from Seoul, I
had to change planes in a major
city in Europe. Then I would

Press conference on Cyprus, Nicocia, May 2006

visit Athens, capital of Greece, which was a major supporter of Greek
Cyprus. As there was no direct flight from Cyprus to Ankara, capital
of Turkey, the sponsoring country of Turkish Cyprus, I had to travel to
Athens, then to Istanbul and change planes again in Istanbul. In addition,
I had to travel to one of the European Community (later European
Union) countries, which served as the chair country of the EC at the
time, which took me to cities like Dublin, Berlin, and Paris. I would then
fly to New York where the U.N. headquarters is located.

It was interesting that, whenever there was some movement in
the deadlock between the two Cypriot entities (the Greek side was
internationally recognized as a government, while the Turkish side
was considered an "authority"), several countries appointed their own
"special representatives." Those countries included Britain, the United
States, Germany, Sweden, and Finland. They did this so that they would

better understand what was going on in Cyprus and so that they could somehow promote their own respective interests in the country.

Interestingly, Russia, which had a strong interest in Cyprus (they were linked by the same religion—Orthodox Christianity and Cyprus was serving as a conduit for Russia's illicit funds, estimated at that time—the mid-1990s—to be approximately 1 billion dollars per month) did not have a significant official diplomatic presence in Cyprus.

By the time I arrived in Cyprus, there had been an uneasy ceasefire by the two sides, which were separated by the United Nations Buffer Zone (also known as the Green Line). The Green Line stretched for 180 kilometers from east to west, varying in width from less than 20 meters to more than 7 kilometers. The zone cuts through the center of Nicosia, the capital of Cyprus, separating the city into southern and northern sections. The presidential offices of both Greek and Turkish Cyprus were less than a couple of kilometers from the line, and I had to cross the line often to meet officials of both sides, although I stayed at a hotel on the Greek side of Nicosia.

Even though the international legal status of the two entities, Greek and Turkish, was not the same, as a U.N. official, I had to show as much impartiality as possible and exercise equal treatment to both sides. The leaders of the two areas, interestingly, had many similarities. President Glafcos Clerides (born in 1919, president 1993-2003) of the Republic of Cyprus and "President" Rauf Denktash (born in 1924, president 1983-2005) of the Turkish Republic of Northern Cyprus, a *de facto* state, were both in their late seventies, English-educated, and had served as barristers in England. They were articulate and eloquent, stubborn and quarrelsome, as they were expected to be as elderly leaders hardened by a long period of struggle.

Occasional mishaps took place in or across the Green Line, including an incident in which a Greek Cypriot refugee was shot in the

Cyprus Mission, June 1996

head by a Turkish officer while trying to remove a Turkish flag from a flagpole in the United Nations Buffer Zone. Although there were charges of murder and defamation of a Turkish flag, the incident did not result in an escalation of violence, instead going to the European Court, which eventually ruled in the Greek victim's favor.

As I was working to rectify the problems of Cyprus, I could not help but think about the country's division and its relevance to the division of Korea. Indeed, there are some peculiar similarities. Historically, Korea was the only country colonized by another Asian country, Japan. Cyprus was the only European country colonized by another European country, Britain. As such, there are still mixed sentiments (some positive but mostly negative) in both Korea and Cyprus toward their respective former colonizers. Korea and Cyprus both have formal armistice lines dividing their territory backed by military force, known as the Military Demarcation Line (MDL) in Korea and the Green Line in Cyprus. The Korean MDL is longer, wider, more closed, and much more heavily guarded. There is also a large economic development gap between the two divided parts.

As in Korea, for reunification, Cyprus needs full cooperation from their respective patron countries, Greece and Turkey. Greece could wield its influence on behalf of its Cypriot brethren by virtue of its membership in the European Union. In fact, in 1999, it succeeded in arranging the accession of (Greek) Cyprus to the European Union without the Turkish part.

Meanwhile, Turkey was providing a life line for Turkish Cyprus by virtue of the fact that it still had an estimated 10,000 troops for defense, economic assistance, and communication (all international telephone calls from Northern Cyprus abroad had to be routed through Turkey). In fact, Turkey was (and still is) the only country in the world to recognize Cyprus as a bona fide government. Turkey also has been tying the fate of Cyprus to the issue of Turkey's accession to the European Union.

What makes the two cases (Korean and Cypriot) quite distinct is the sociological and historical background of their division. Cyprus was divided as a result of ethnic conflict between the Greek Cypriots and Turkish Cypriots while Korea was divided by the geopolitics of the United States and the Soviet Union. Some Cypriots of both sides claim that the expression "ethnic cleansing" was first used in connection with the Cyprus situation. Today, more than half of the 200,000 residents in northern Turkish Cyprus are not even original Cypriots, but are settlers who came to Cyprus from Anatolia after 1974. There is little commonality between the southern and northern Cypriot people to bring them together but many grievances and animosity to separate them. By contrast, one still hears North and South Koreans chanting "we are one people," and for the most part there is no animosity between them at the people's level.

What animosity that remains from the struggle and mutual slaughter of the Korean War almost seven decades ago is directed towards the former government leaders of the time. Many older South Koreans, especially those who came from the North, still resent North Korea's Kim dynasty, which started the devastating Korean War, continues to threaten the South with nuclear weapons and provocations, and oppresses its own people. The division has been so long and so complete in Korea, and the people of the South and North have had such little direct contact.

Another difference is that both Koreas are armed to the teeth (including North Korea's nuclear weapons) for security, deterrence, or as a possible means to take over the other side. In contrast, Greek Cyprus is not necessarily concerned about the military aggressiveness of Turkish Cyprus, which also does not really worry about a military invasion by Greek Cyprus.

During my watch as the Special Representative of the Secretary-General (SRSG), no major mishap occurred at the border or between the two sides, but neither were there any major breakthroughs. As I was taking too much time away from my university responsibilities without taking a leave of absence and was exhausted from traveling so many miles with meager results, I took the opportunity of the transition from Boutros-Ghali to Kofi Annan as secretary-general and resigned my U.N. post for Cyprus.

Rwanda: Independent Enquiry Commission on the 1994 Genocide in Rwanda

In mid-March 1999, I received a letter from U.N. Secretary-General Kofi Annan, asking me to join a three-person commission of inquiry on the 1994 Rwanda genocide. The commission consisted of the former prime minister of Sweden Ingvar Carlsson, who would serve as chairman of the group, Lieutenant General Rufus M. Kupolati of Nigeria, and me. The independent commission of inquiry was to look into the actions of the U.N. at the time of the genocide.

The commission was formed to address the continuing controversy over the U.N.'s presumably inadequate actions during the genocide. These ethnic killings resulted in more than 800,000 deaths of mostly Tutsis in just over one hundred days. This happened despite the presence of a U.N. peacekeeping force named the United Nations Assistance Mission for Rwanda (UNAMIR). As the U.N. peacekeeping operation was under the purview of then Assistant Secretary-General of the United Nations Kofi Annan, who headed the U.N. Department of Peacekeeping Operations (DPKO), his role in dealing with the genocide continued to be a subject of controversy and criticism, even after he became the secretary-general. One way or the other, the secretary-general obviously sought to leave the controversy behind him.

For more than eight months, until the end of December, the commission worked tirelessly, going through U.N. documents (mostly cables that went back and forth between the headquarters and the field). We visited not only Rwanda, but also neighboring countries in Africa like Uganda and Tanzania, Europe (Belgium and France had a substantial military presence in Rwanda), and the United States (which played a key role as a leading member of the Security Council P-5). We also interviewed key human rights organizations such as Human Rights Watch and the International Red Cross, which played a critical role in saving lives during the genocide under extremely hazardous circumstances. In our work, we were more than ably assisted by the Commission of Inquiry's two special advisers, Elinor Hammarskjold of Sweden (a Swedish diplomat who was also a granddaughter of former U.N. Secretary-General Dag Hammarskjold) and Professor Lee Shin-

From left to right: Ms. Hammarskjold; Gen. Kupolati,
Former Prime Minister Carlsson, author

wha of Korea University.

The Rwanda genocide of 1994 took the lives of some 20 percent of the total population and 70 percent of the Tutsi Rwandans. The number killed in the genocide was the third largest in the twentieth century, after the six million Jews killed by Nazi Germany in the Holocaust and two million Cambodians killed by the Khmer Rouge in the 1970s. The number of lost lives during the 100-day period meant that around 10,000 people were killed every day—400 people every hour, seven people every minute.

Preparations for the genocide were made at the government level. At the time the genocide began, there was ethnic friction between the majority Hutus and minority Tutsis, and some 30,000 non-military Hutus were armed with AK-47 rifles and grenades. There were signs of a possible "ethnic cleansing" operation in Rwanda, a former colony of Belgium, before it began in March 1994, but no measures were taken by the U.N. or countries such as Belgium, France, or the United States, which had the means to intervene. France, which had an interest in maintaining Rwanda as a Francophone country and had supported the Hutu government of Juvénal Habyarimana, generally favored the Hutus in the ethnic conflict. Belgium, the former colonial ruler of Rwanda, had troops in the country but was mainly interested in protecting its own nationals rather than preventing or stopping the genocide. The United States, which had lost 15 U.S. soldiers in Somalia the year before, was in no mood to intervene in Rwanda at the time.

Even after the genocide began in mid-April 1994, the major powers, including the United States, refrained from characterizing what was happening as a "genocide," as doing so would have legally obligated them to intervene under the provisions of the Convention on the Prevention and Punishment of the Crime of Genocide that was concluded in 1948.

The United Nations, which refrained from taking more proactive measures, could not escape blame. Despite warnings given to the headquarters from the UNAMIR commander regarding the amassing of weapons and the conspiracy for the killings, the leadership in New York only gave constraining orders. The peacekeeping force was forbidden from acting against the conspirators or actively stopping the genocide once it began. The reason was that intervening in the ethnic killing was beyond UNAMIR's mandate, and the U.N. had not received a green light to act from the P-5 countries.

In fact, once the killings began, the U.N. decided to withdraw all peacekeeping forces from Rwanda except a contingent of 270. The U.N. assumed the position of an onlooker, showcasing their unwillingness to actively stop a large-scale slaughter in the name of remaining neutral between the warring parties. Leaders of major countries were more worried about the likelihood of domestic political criticism should their intervention result in casualties. As a result, no member country, especially those of the Security Council P-5, chose to intervene in a country with which they saw no direct link to their "national interest."

There were even accusations that the presence of the U.N. peacekeeping force served as a cause for more victims to be killed. They cited the case in which hundreds of Tutsis gathered in a stadium expecting to be protected by U.N. peacekeepers, only to be killed en masse with grenades and machetes.

Years after the genocide ended and order was restored, President Clinton visited Rwanda's capital Kigali in remembrance of the victims and to apologize to the survivors. He pledged that such a tragedy would not be repeated. However, since then, when other genocidal acts have occurred in places such as Darfur and Sudan, the outside world remained just as inactive as it was in the case of the Rwanda genocide.

During the course of the genocide and afterwards, the organizations which rendered critical help and assistance to victims were non-governmental organizations (NGOs) such as Human Rights Watch and the International Red Cross. The movie "Hotel Rwanda" was a dramatic and moving documentation of the brave and humanitarian acts of hotelier Paul Rusesabagina, a Hutu, and his wife Tatiana, who saved nearly 1,300 refugees by providing shelter and a hideout in the besieged Hotel des Mille Collines in Kigali.

The genocide ended some 100 days after it began when the Tutsi's Rwanda Patriotic Front, led by Paul Kagame, which had been armed and trained in neighboring Uganda, advanced into Rwanda and defeated the Hutu regime. Even though the government of Paul Kagame, who was installed as Rwanda's president, took over all of Rwanda and drove out the remnants of the Hutu regime, there were still the difficult tasks of rounding up and punishing the perpetrators of the genocide, reconciling warring ethnic groups, reconstructing the destroyed economy, and rehabilitating the shattered social fabric. At the international level, there

were the tasks of trying the culprits, realizing justice, and rebuilding
capabilities and structures (including the U.N. peacekeeping force) for
more effective interventions to protect human lives and rights across
national boundaries in the future.

After eight months of intensive work, on December 15, 1999,
the U.N. Independent Commission of Inquiry on the 1994 Rwanda
genocide submitted a formal report on its findings, the gist of which is as
follows:[12]

"The international community did not prevent the genocide, nor
did it stop the killing once the genocide had begun. This failure has
left deep wounds within Rwandan society, and in the relationship
between Rwanda and the international community, in particular
the United Nations. These are wounds which need to be healed, for
the sake of the people of Rwanda and for the sake of the United
Nations. Establishing the truth is necessary for Rwanda, for the
United Nations and also for all those, wherever they may live, who
are at risk of becoming victims of genocide in the future.

The failure by the United Nations to prevent, and subsequently,
to stop the genocide in Rwanda was a failure by the United
Nations system as a whole. The fundamental failure was the lack
of resources and political commitment devoted to developments
in Rwanda and to the United Nations presence there. There was a
persistent lack of political will by Member States to act, or to act
with enough assertiveness. This lack of political will affected the
response by the Secretariat and decision-making by the Security
Council, but was also evident in the recurrent difficulties to get the
necessary troops for the United Nations Assistance Mission for

---

12 *Report of the Independent Inquiry into the Actions of the United Nations During the 1994
Genocide in Rwanda* (Report of the United Nations, December 15, 1999).

Rwanda (UNAMIR). Finally, although UNAMIR suffered from a chronic lack of resources and political priority, it must also be said that serious mistakes were made with those resources which were at the disposal of the United Nations."

The report identified the following failures, short-comings and mistakes in U.N.'s response to the 1994 crisis in Rwanda.

1. The overriding failure

The overriding failure in the response of the United Nations before and during the genocide in Rwanda can be summarized as a lack of resources and a lack of will to take on the commitment which would have been necessary to prevent or to stop the genocide. UNAMIR, the main component of the United Nations presence in Rwanda, was not planned, dimensioned, deployed or instructed in a way which provided for a proactive and assertive role in dealing with a peace process in serious trouble.

2. The inadequacy of UNAMIR's mandate

The decisions taken with respect to the scope of the initial mandate of UNAMIR were an underlying factor in the failure of the mission to prevent or stop the genocide in Rwanda. The planning process failed to take into account remaining serious tensions which had not been solved in the agreements between the parties.

3. The implementation of the mandate

UNAMIR's mandate was cautious in its conception; it was to become equally so in its application on the ground. Headquarters consistently decided to apply the mandate in a manner which would preserve a neutral role of UNAMIR under a traditional peacekeeping mandate. This was the scope of action that was perceived to have support in the Security Council. Despite facing a deteriorating security situation which would have motivated a more assertive and preventive role for the United Nations, no steps were taken to adjust the mandate to the reality of the needs in Rwanda.

4. Failure to respond to the genocide

The correspondence between UNAMIR and Headquarters during the hours and days after the plane crash shows a force in disarray, with little intelligence about the true nature of what is happening and what political and military forces are at play, with no clear direction and with problems even communicating among its own contingents. The mission was under rules of engagement not to use force except in self defence. It had taken upon itself to protect politicians, but then in certain cases did not do so in the face of threats by the militia. Civilians were drawn to UNAMIR posts but the mission proved incapable of sustaining protection of them.

5. Failure to recognize the mass murder as "genocide"

Key members of the International Community failed to acknowledge that the mass murder being pursued in front of global media was a genocide. The main reason was that, according to the 1948 Convention against Genocide, recognition of what was occurring in Rwanda was a genocide brought with it a key international obligation to act in order to stop the killing. The delay in identifying the events in Rwanda as a genocide was a failure by the Security Council. The reluctance by some States to use the term genocide was motivated by a lack of will to act, which is deplorable.

6. Peacekeeping overburdened: inadequate resources and

logistics

Rwanda was to prove a turning point in United Nations peacekeeping, and came to symbolize a lack of will to commit to peacekeeping, and above all, to take risks in the field. UNAMIR came about following a dramatic expansion of the number of peacekeeping troops in the field after the end of the Cold War. However, by the second half of 1993, the enthusiasm for United Nations peacekeeping of previous years was on the wane among key member states, the capacity of the Secretariat, in particular the DPKO, to administer the approximately 70,000 peacekeepers wearing blue berets was overstretched, and several existing operations were facing severe difficulties.

7. The shadow of Somalia

It has often been said that UNAMIR was an operation which was created in the shadow of Somalia. In particular the deaths of the Pakistani and US peacekeepers in Somalia in 1993 had a deep effect on the attitude towards the conduct of peacekeeping operations.

8. Focus on achieving a cease-fire

The Inquiry finds it disturbing that records of meetings between members of the Secretariat, including the Secretary-General, with officials of the so-called Interim Government show a continued emphasis on a cease-fire, more than the moral outrage against the massacres, which was growing in the international community.

9. Lack of analytical capacity

A problem in the United Nations response to the situation in Rwanda was the weaknesses apparent in the capacity for political analysis, in particular within UNAMIR, but also at Headquarters. With respect to UNAMIR, a key problem identified by the Force Commander in an interview with the Inquiry was the weak political representation in the reconnaissance mission to Rwanda in August 1993 and the lack of real understanding the team had about the underlying political realities of the Rwandan peace process.

10. The lack of political will of Member States

Another reason for the main failure of the international community in Rwanda was the lack of political will to give UNAMIR the personnel and materiel resources the mission needed. Even after the Security Council decided to act to try and stop the killing, and reversed its decision to reduce UNAMIR, the problems that the Secretariat had faced since UNAMIR's inception in getting contributions of troops from Member States persisted. This was the case throughout in May and June during the urgent attempts to set up UNAMIR II.

11. Failure to protect political leaders

UNAMIR was tasked with the protection of a number of politicians who were of key importance to the implementation of the Arusha Agreement. Moderate and opposition politicians quickly became targets as violence started after the crash of the Presidential plane. Some of them were saved, among them the Prime Minister Designate, Mr Twagiramungu. A number of others, however, were killed by members of the Presidential Guards and elements of the Rwandese army. In these cases, UNAMIR did not succeed in providing the protection these personalities required.

12. Failure to protect civilians

Considerable efforts were made by members of UNAMIR, sometimes at risk to themselves, to provide protection to civilians at risk during the massacres. However, there do not seem to have been conscious and consistent orders down the chain of command on this issue. During the early days of the genocide, thousands of civilians congregated in places where UN troops were stationed. Tragically, there is evidence that in certain instances, the trust placed in UNAMIR by civilians left them in a situation of greater risk when the UN troops withdrew than they would have been otherwise.

13. Failure to protect national staff

It is a tragic aspect of modern conflict that national staff of the United Nations as well as other humanitarian personnel are increasingly the targets of violence during armed conflict. The genocide in Rwanda took its toll among the personnel of the United Nations: fourteen peacekeepers and a number of local civilian staff were brutally killed.

14. National evacuations: international troops in different roles

The rapid deployment of the national contingents to evacuate expatriates from Kigali saved lives among the expatriate community. Nonetheless, the lack of coordination on the ground with the United Nations before the operations is a matter of concern. The leadership of UNAMIR, or of the Secretariat, should have been better informed about the evacuations being planned.

15. Rwanda as a member of the Security Council

The fact that Rwanda, represented by the Habyarimana

government, was a member of the Security Council from January 1994 was a problem in the Security Council's handling of the Rwanda issue. In effect, one of the parties to the Arusha Peace Agreement had full access to the discussions of the Council and had the opportunity to try to influence decision-making in the Council on its own behalf. That a party to a conflict on the agenda of the Council, which was the host country of a peacekeeping operation, later subject to an arms embargo imposed by the body of which it was a member, shows the damaging effect of Rwanda's membership on the Council.

The Commission of Inquiry made the following specific recommendations.

1. "The Secretary-General should initiate an action plan to prevent genocide involving the whole UN system, and aiming to provide input to the World Conference against Racism, Racial Discrimination, Xenophobia and Related Intolerance in 2001.
2. Renewed efforts should be made to improve the capacity of the UN in the field of peacekeeping, including the availability of resources: political momentum for action should be mobilized at the Millennium Summit and Assembly. In each peacekeeping operation it should be clear which Rules of Engagement apply.
3. The United Nations - and in particular the Security Council and troop contributing countries - must be prepared to act to prevent acts of genocide or gross violations of human rights wherever they may take place. The political will to act should not be subject to different standards.

4. The early warning capacity of the United Nations needs to be improved, through better cooperation with outside actors including NGOs and academics, as well as within the Secretariat.

5. Efforts need to be made to improve the protection of civilians in conflict situations.

6. Further improvements in the security of UN and associated personnel, including local staff, are necessary. Consideration should be given to changing existing rules to enable the evacuation of national staff from crisis areas.

7. Cooperation between officials responsible for the security of different categories of staff in the field needs to be ensured.

8. National evacuation operations must be coordinated with UN missions on the ground.

9. The United Nations should acknowledge its part of the responsibility for not having done enough to prevent or stop the genocide in Rwanda. The Secretary-General should actively seek ways to launch a new beginning in the relationship between the United Nations and Rwanda."

Conclusions

"The Independent Inquiry finds that the response of the United Nations before and during the 1994 genocide in Rwanda failed in a number of fundamental respects. The responsibility for the failings of the United Nations to prevent and stop the genocide in Rwanda lies with a number of different actors, in particular the Secretary-General, the Secretariat, the Security Council, UNAMIR and the broader membership of the United Nations. This international responsibility is one which warrants a clear apology by the Organization and by Member States concerned to the Rwandese people. As to the responsibility of those Rwandans who planned, incited and carried out the genocide against their countrymen, continued efforts must be made to bring them to justice - at the International Criminal Tribunal for Rwanda and nationally in Rwanda."

The 1994 Rwanda Genocide and ethnic mass killings in other parts of the world are indicative of the dilemma the world faces between the responsibility to protect what is known as individual sovereignty and the maintenance of respect for national sovereignty. While the former involves the individual's right to life and human dignity and the state's responsibility to protect such rights, the latter is related to the prohibition in international law of the threat or use of force against political independence of any state (Article 2.4 of the United Nations Charter).

But the relatively frequent occurrence of genocide, particularly in the 20th century, including the Nazi massacre of the Jews, mass killing in Cambodia, "ethnic cleansing" in Srebrenica and Darfur, and the Rwanda genocide, are reminders that genocide will not disappear from the earth and will likely to continue to haunt the world in the decades and perhaps centuries to come. The inhumane oppression and exclusion of minorities are still being witnessed in the ongoing plight of the Rohingya people in Myanmar.

In a less dramatic, but no less tragic way, it is also reflected in the triumph in many presumably civilized countries of nativistic nationalism, racism, and parochialism over universalism, internationalism, and humanitarianism. In many advanced countries, the liberal, international, and domestic order that seemed to be universally accepted after the Second World War, seems to be in danger of being replaced by a less liberal, if not completely illiberal, order.

However, even in the name of majoritarian democracy, basic

human rights, particularly the right to life, equality, liberty, and human dignity, cannot and should not be deprived or suppressed. The world has to find a way to protect these rights, which can be called "individual sovereignty," even if by doing so some aspects of "national sovereignty" are infringed upon. The work of the commission of inquiry was important in highlighting the complex nature of the non-traditional security challenges that are faced by the global community in the 21st century. During the course of our work over an intense eight-month period, each of the commissioners was forced to deeply consider the nature of the problems and to seek potential solutions or remedies for them in the future.

East Asian Vision Group (EAVG)

In December 1999, I was asked by the South Korean Foreign Ministry to join the East Asian Vision Group (EAVG), a 1.5-track advisory group with 26 representatives charged with charting a roadmap to further regional cooperation and community-building in the East Asian region. At the time, the South Korean government was keen on taking a leadership role in regional community-building for two reasons. One was that, as people became more aware of the relative rise of the economic power of East Asia, they became more interested in the prospect of cooperation and community-building in the region. The second reason was more political. President Kim Dae-Jung, who was elected in 1998 on a liberal and globalist platform, was intent on becoming not only a national leader, but a leader of regional and international stature. For him, staking a claim as a regional advocate of

Asia-Pacific Round Table, Monterey, California, 2006. Participants include: George Schultz, U.S.A (front row, third from left); Bill Bradley, U.S.A (standing, second from left); George Yeo, Singapore (standing, second from right); Gareth Evans, Australia (standing, first on the right); author (sitting, in front row, first on the right)

cooperation and integration was a ticket to international recognition.[13]

In our year-long discussion and drafting of the EAVG report, we agreed on the need to forge closer economic cooperation, including freer trade and financial unions, such as the Chiang Mai Initiative, as well as cooperation on issues of education, culture, energy, and environment. But we also had disagreements on a number of other issues. They included whether to use the word "community" in our group name. At the time, the European Economic Community (EEC) had become the European Union and was on the way to becoming the fully integrated EU of today. The EEC was created by the Treaty of Rome in 1957. In 1993, the EEC was incorporated and renamed the European Union. In 2009, the EU's institutions were absorbed into a wider framework.

---

13   See The East Asia Vision Group Report, "Toward an East Asian Community: Region of Peace, Prosperity and Progress," October 31, 1999.

Also at that time, APEC could not agree on a name like "organization," "community," or "union." It thus ended up as a "cooperation" which is not even a proper noun. In EAVG, we finally agreed to use the term "community," but only under the condition that we do not use the capital "C" for East Asian Community. However, nobody objected when we used a capital "C" in the title of our report, which was "Toward an East Asian Community."

There were other disagreements as well. We disagreed over to what extent the group would delve into non-economic (namely political and security) matters. Some countries even opposed the use of the term "human security." Another issue of contention was to what extent the sanctity or "centrality" of ASEAN could be affected in the interest of East Asian integration. For example, we agreed to propose an East Asian Summit (EAS) to be held in addition to the annual ASEAN Plus Three (APT) Ministers' meetings. But members of the ASEAN countries insisted that the agenda of such a summit should be determined by ASEAN and that its venue should rotate within ASEAN countries.

I introduce this piece of history, not to be funny or entertaining, but to illustrate how the creation and nurturing of a regional community in East Asia remains an important but difficult task.

EAS v. ASEAN +3?

During the last quarter of the twentieth century, there were two competing strands of international and regional relations in East Asia. One was the pull toward regional integration and cooperation. The other was the continuing trend toward big power and nation-centered realpolitik. The first strand of emphasizing multilateralism and international cooperation in Asia was inspired by the successful example of the European Community (which became the European Union). This strand found expression in the name of Asia-Pacific or the East Asian Community and could be considered an idealistic expression of regionalism and international cooperation. The second strand, emphasizing the dominance of geopolitics, sought (and still seeks) recognition of the continuing dominance of what political scientists call "realism" in East Asian international relations. If the first strand was born out of the recognition that economic cooperation is both necessary and desirable in East Asia, the second was formulated because competition among major powers in the region continued to shape interests and inform national security considerations.

On the surface, much has been happening on the regional cooperation/integration front.The EAS, has been held since its inception in 2005 and now includes 17 countries, including ASEAN, China, Japan, South Korea, the United States, Russia, India, and Australia. APEC has been holding the Asia Pacific regional economic leaders' meetings, focusing on topics such as regional economic integration, monetary cooperation, and the Free Trade Area of the Asia-Pacific (FTAAP).

With the APT summit meetings and the EAS being held on an annual basis, East Asian community-building seems to be moving toward closer regional cooperation and integration. The EAS, as it has turned out, is an *addition* to the APT summit, which was launched in 1997. It is neither a replacement for nor an evolution of what was originally envisaged. However, the old dilemma that has dogged the promoters of the East Asian community still remains: How do we reconcile the community with Asia-Pacific regionalism, particularly embodied in APEC? How does EAS avoid being redundant or competing with either ASEAN Plus Three or the APEC summit? A corollary question is how and to what extent the United States can and should be engaged in the regionalism movement in East Asia. Being unable to give a clear-cut answer to these questions, the major players of the region are faced with their own respective dilemmas, whether to throw their weight in favor of rapid community-building, take a passive stance, or actively oppose it.

The United States, although it has joined the EAS, remains outside of the APT group and used to have more misgivings than support for an East Asian grouping. The U.S. worried that an East Asian community would dilute the meaning and effectiveness of Asia-Pacific cooperation. It was also concerned that East Asia might develop into a group dominated by Chinese influence. The U.S. strongly opposed the EAEC (East Asian Economic Caucus) proposal made by the Malaysian Prime Minister Mohammed Mahatir in the early 1990s. During the intervening years, when de facto East Asian summits were held under the name of ASEAN Plus Three, the U.S. seemed rather undecided whether to support it, simply wait and see, or actively oppose it. In the end, it decided to join the ASEAN-initiated Treaty of Amity and Cooperation (TAC), work on FTAs with such countries like Singapore and South Korea, and participate in the EAS. There is a growing awareness among U.S. experts and policymakers that regional integration might proceed even without the U.S., and hence there is an expressed desire to be involved. Nonetheless, the U.S. still lacks a well-articulated policy regarding an East Asia community.

Japan's dilemma was that it had reasons to actively participate in EAS and, at the same time, keep pace with the steady but slow development of East Asian regionalism. Japan did not want to leave the field open for countries like China to take the lead without Japan being actively involved in East Asian community-building. This revolved around Japan's desire to maintain a balance and promote its own interests through close cooperation with ASEAN and the rest of East Asia. On the other hand, Japan had to be conscious about the attitudes of its closest ally, the U.S. Hence, it hoped to find a way to facilitate

U.S. engagement in East Asian regionalization while Japan was actively participating in regional community-building. Another dilemma that Japan had was related to its sometimes troubled relations with its Northeast Asian neighbors, particularly China and South Korea, over the issue of how to deal with the past. Japan has found it difficult to promote regional cooperation while still facing lingering disputes with its closest neighbors. To the credit of the recent Japanese prime ministers, Japan has begun to mend fences with China and South Korea, the two countries whose relationship had been damaged by their predecessor's lack of sensitivity.

South Korea has a dilemma of its own—the dilemma of wishing to be a core member of the larger Asia-Pacific on the one hand while still playing the linchpin role in East Asia between big and small countries, developed and developing economies, and continental (China) and maritime (Japan) powers. To date, its most noteworthy contribution to East Asian regionalism has been its partly successful proposal to turn the APT summit into the EAS. It was only partly successful, because the EAS has been added onto, not replaced, the APT summit. If such a replacement occurred, the change of the name would be more than semantics. It would give China, Japan, and South Korea the opportunity to play a key role, together with ASEAN, in the agenda and priority setting of the summit meeting. The three countries would have also had the opportunity to host the summit meetings. Now that South Korea has become a member of the G-20, and has even assumed a leadership role in the exercise known as the "premier summit" for the world economy, it can feel relaxed about the regional East Asia community movement, whether initiatives are taken by Japan, China, or ASEAN.

ASEAN's main dilemma is that, as in the case of APEC, if a larger pan-regional grouping is formed, ASEAN's own integrity might be affected. ASEAN would also be wary of sharing the leadership role with

Northeast Asian countries, particularly China and Japan, which are far larger and stronger members of the region. ASEAN's answer to both of these dilemmas seems to have been to open the East Asia Summit to additional countries from outside of East Asia. Later on, this could have the effect of diluting East Asian coherence, which might compete with Southeast Asia's own, and also serve as a counter-weight to each or all of the Northeast Asian countries. Thus, ASEAN has chosen to keep the APT summit as the "main vehicle" of East Asian cooperation.

China's dilemma relating to the EAS is perhaps the smallest. China is pursuing what amounts to a good neighbor policy vis-à-vis Southeast Asia, the Korean Peninsula, and until the Senkaku/Diaoyu Island controversy, Japan as well. China has already concluded an FTA with ASEAN. It took a leadership role in the Six-Party Talks aimed at resolving the North Korean nuclear issue, although, for more than fifteen years, since 2005, the Six-Party Talks has been in a serious limbo. China, which supported the idea of the East Asia Summit with the expectation of playing a dominant role, has been a relative "purist" in wanting to limit the membership of EAS to the original ten plus three East Asian countries. China was therefore disappointed with the expansion and thus dilution of the concept of East Asia, and has lost some enthusiasm with the exercise.

China's other dilemma is related to the scope of regionalism, specifically, whether to include the subject of security in regional cooperation. China has resisted including the subject of security in APEC, which includes both Taiwan (in the name of Chinese Taipei) and Hong Kong. Until recently, APEC's agenda has been confined to trade, investment, technology, environment, and other economic and functional fields. Of late, however, APEC found a way to bring security subjects into the agenda, in the name of "human security." China has shown reluctance to include the subject of conventional security, in the

agendas of APT, the EAS, or in bilateral summits that accompany the
APT summit.

Problems with EAS

Even as the EAS continues to be held on an annual basis and is
making progress, there are too many unresolved issues and loose ends.
One key issue is the relationship between the APT summit and EAS.
The current APT cooperative system continues to develop into an
increasingly structured mechanism. ASEAN tends to regard EAS as a
sort of "post-APT" dialogue forum. This leads to the question of which
summit (APT or EAS) will be charged with the task of creating an East
Asian community. The majority of ASEAN countries seem to espouse
an "APT centric" approach. They argue that the question of forming
an East Asian community should be covered in the APT summit, not in
EAS.

Other countries, such as Japan and Australia, tend to hold the
position that EAS should be involved with issues such as the creation
of an East Asian community. They stress that APT should be a forum
to explore functional cooperation, while EAS should be a forum for
conceptual and strategic issues, such as peace and development.

The rise of China's economic prowess, the willingness of China
to use its economic leverage for diplomatic and political purposes, the
uncertainties related to the future of North Korea and its continuing
nuclear program, the competition between TPP and RCEP, the emerging
alignments and alliance systems with the United States and China as
their respective lynchpins—all of these geopolitical elements make
community-building in East Asia problematic. Furthermore, the
continuing relevance of geopolitics in East Asia makes the role of the

United States, still unrivaled militarily, all the more critical. It has played an indispensable role in East Asian development, economic and security crises, and natural disasters.

Another major factor in the evolution of East Asian cooperation is the relationship between China and the United States. In the post-Cold War era, China-U.S. relations have consisted of both cooperation and competition. In military affairs, however, there is more competition than cooperation. The U.S. is concerned about China's growing defense budget, which they estimate to be much more than what China has publicly admitted.

Similarly, China seeks to act as a counterbalance to the U.S. military presence in Asia. A recent Chinese defense white paper stated that the U.S. has increased its strategic attention to and input in the Asia-Pacific region, further consolidating its military alliances, adjusting its military deployment and enhancing its military capabilities. China is unhappy about the large and continued weapons sales from the U.S. to Taiwan, as well as U.S.-led military exercises around Chinese waters. China complains about the missile defense systems that the U.S. is building. The U.S., meanwhile, opposes China's power extension in the South China Sea.

Yet, in the economic arena, China and the United States are inexorably tied to each other and interdependent. The U.S. is China's largest trading partner and China is one of the largest trading partners of the U.S. Any downturn in the U.S. economy represents a direct and serious loss to the Chinese economy and vice versa. A trade war between them will also bring havoc to both countries' economy.

In Europe, serious problems are hampering smooth regional integration. The EU cannot find a solution to the migrant problem. Greece talks about Grexit, while Britain pursues an effective Brexit. All of these problems give pause to those who have been promoting East

Asian integration, cooperation, and community-building.

Where Do We Go From Here?

When Europe was promoting regional integration, it had three closely interrelated purposes. First, Europe wished to evolve into a regional community, thereby achieving internal peace and common prosperity; second, community-building was a means to build an effective counter to the looming Soviet threat; and third, regional integration dealt with the "German question," which required the harnessing and incorporating of Germany, divided or unified.

The United States supported European community-building as it shared with Europe the objectives of countering Soviet power and incorporating Germany into a larger Europe. The U.S. was linked to Europe through NATO, which meant there was no particular compulsion for the U.S. to be involved in European community-building.

Needless to say, the circumstances are quite different in East Asia. However, if there is a need to harness the larger powers in East Asia, i.e., China and Japan, and incorporate them into a larger regional grouping, an East Asian community would be the appropriate mechanism to do so. This will be desirable not only for the countries in the region, but also for the U.S. The fact that the U.S. is linked to East Asia through APEC should be a good reason to welcome the emergence of an East Asian community.

In sum, as we discuss an East Asian community (either with a small c or a capital C), we can think about it as a sort of organic, naturally emerging phenomenon or as a community-building process forged by official actions. One may say that a community is already emerging in East Asia, primarily as the result of intensified economic and social interactions and interdependencies. In this scenario, a community will define itself on the basis of what the members have in common, and what they strive for together.

Does this lend the impression that we are trending toward an East Asian Community? Or are they more an indication that the East Asian Community concept faces major obstacles, particularly in the form of rising nationalism among the major countries in Northeast Asia?

For the moment, I think the appropriate response, if not the answer, can be found in looking closely into the nature of the "emerging community," in addition to the conscious attempts at institutional community-building. Perhaps we should not be too ambitious or hasty with our desire for regional community-building. The institutionally driven moves toward an East Asian community can certainly enhance the forces that are naturally emerging around the region, in spite of the obstacles that remain. Nonetheless, at the moment, the naturally emerging community outpacing the institutional one seems to be carrying the day.

Saving Multilateralism in a Unilateral World

Today we are seeing disruptions and changes in our way of life at an unprecedented rate and at all different levels. Much of this has to do with things that we associate with globalization—free trade, advanced technology, and instantaneous digital communication methods. These developments were facilitated and supported by the post-World War II liberal world order. Many experts once thought that these changes represented a march toward progress (i.e. Thomas Friedman in *The World Is Flat*). We also believed that these processes would help redistribute resources and close the gap between the haves and the have-nots across the globe.

There have been many positive outcomes from these changes. But, unfortunately in the aftermath of the Brexit vote, the 2016 U.S. election, and in the midst of growing nationalist movements around the world, we can also see more clearly that there are large groups of people who feel negatively affected by the changes. The backlash against globalization and "elite politics" has some arguing that the liberal order is facing collapse.

I do not believe that the liberal order will collapse easily, but it is evident that it is facing significant challenges. If we do not deal effectively with these challenges, then I fear there will be a return to a more illiberal world order, one that is less stable and less peaceful. That is why discussing these challenges and "updating" post-World War II rules for multilateral cooperation is so important. I would like to pose the following question: "Why is it necessary for us to update the rules for multilateral cooperation?"

I see three possible reasons. First, to make the rules more consistent with the change from a hegemonic or oligarchic order to a world where power is more diffused. Second, to make it more palatable to the still reigning dominant power, the United States, whose leadership seems to be less supportive of multilateralism than in the past. Finally, to integrate rising powers into the world order.

But is it too late to think about updating post-World War II rules for multilateralism? As it happens, I think the most urgent issue we have to address today is not so much how to update and change the rules as how to deal with the challenges multilateralism is facing today from unilateralist impulses, nativistic nationalism, and anti-globalism—all of which amount to anti-multilateralism.

Looking back, multilateral institutions in the post-World War II period owe their creation and growth to three factors: 1) The recognition, by the dominant power and the lesser powers alike, of their shared interest in achieving common goals through multilateralism; 2) A degree of idealism to achieve such objectives as peace and human well-being through multilateral institutions; and 3) The acknowledgment of the existence of common public goods, such as financial stability, environmental protection, and freedom of the seas.

In the post-World War II period, the growth of multilateralism was possible because a bargain was made between the dominant power, the U.S., and other countries, which included both middle and small powers. In such a bargain, the dominant state succeeds in reducing its enforcement costs and the weaker states gain opportunities to help influence the system.

In the U.S., the Trump Administration seems to be skeptical of the utility of multilateralism. It pulled out of the Trans-Pacific Partnership (TPP) agreement, wants to revise the North Atlantic Free Trade Agreement (NAFTA), plans to reduce financial contribution to the U.N., and seems to be equivocal about NATO. In Europe, starting with Brexit, ultra-conservative and nationalist political forces seem to be on the ascendency. In France's last presidential election, they came very close to electing a candidate who could be described as anti-Europe.

How do we account for the rise of anti-globalization and sentiments skeptical of multilateralism? First, in the aftermath of the changes in recent decades, there is misplacement of blame, either deliberate or genuine, for the malaises at home, including unemployment and the income gap. Second, such blame invokes an identity crisis for many, which in turn makes them find enemies and scapegoats among certain ethnic, racial, or religious groups and cling to their own ethnic or religious identity. In each case, there are leaders who take political advantage of such identity disorientation, fear, and anger. By drawing on the sentiments of fear and anger, leaders can more easily turn international relations into a zero-sum game rather than a positive-sum game. The search for shared ideals and public goods becomes difficult, if not impossible.

Even at the turn of the 21st century, when the U.S. seemed to enjoy what amounted to rising unipolarity, the incentives for multipolarity were maintained. The George W. Bush administration sometimes resorted to unilateralism, but did not threaten the maintenance of multipolar arrangements in both security and economic spheres.

Like most other nations, the U.S. has a strong sense of nationalism. Since the end of the Second World War, the U.S. has led and supported multilateralism, partly because of civic nationalism based on democratic institutions and ideals. Today, however, there are many observers who are concerned about the rise of what the *New York Times* columnist David Brooks calls "ethnic nationalism." According to Professor John Ikenberry of Princeton University, the American national identity did not used to be based on ethnic or religious particularism but was founded on a more general set of agreed-upon and normatively appealing principles. Now, the priorities seem to be reversing themselves.

So, what will be the consequences of the weakening, if not abandoning, of multilateralism? From the U.S.' point of view, moving away from multilateralism and the insistence on unilateralism and bilateralism will bring about its own isolation and strengthen the coalitions of rival states and its competitors' positions.

Other states will also have much to lose in terms of their immediate security and economic interests, not to speak of idealism and global public goods. There is also the danger of international relations becoming more power-based than rule-based.

Coming back to the original question, how to update post-World War II rules for multilateral cooperation, it seems that, of the rules that are being contested, three areas stand out: 1) the question of sovereignty and non-intervention; 2) integration of rising powers into the world order; and 3) safeguarding access to the open global commons, such as the maritime, aerospace, and cyberspace domains.

The first question, of sovereignty and non-intervention, involves not only balancing what former U.N. Secretary-General Kofi Annan called "state sovereignty and individual sovereignty," but also promoting human rights and democracy. The second question, of integrating rising powers into the world order, involves addressing the stratified structure of the U.N. Security Council, which is related to veto power and the permanent membership of the "P-5" countries. It also involves adjusting the rules to account for the redistribution of power and roles of various states and institutions in global economics. The third question, of access to the open global commons, involves adjusting to rapid technological innovation while coping with clashing territorial claims that are still prevalent, particularly in Asia.

The problem with changing rules is that these changes will require the weakening of the dominant powers' control and influence over powerful multilateral organizations. It will also require the consent of the dominant powers, who might have much to lose. The clash between the interests of the status quo and revisionist powers is well demonstrated in the Non-Proliferation Treaty (NPT) review conferences that take place every five years.

Updating or changing rules is a lofty but truly difficult goal. But we must consider all options that will help us to strengthen the positive effects of multilateral cooperation and to prevent the collapse of the liberal order. If we do not have the courage to deal with challenges to the current international system, then we may find ourselves returning to a time when our world was embroiled in conflict, with less prosperity and security for all people.

In the midst of great change, we should encourage world leaders not to move away from multilateralism, but to find creative and comprehensive solutions to economic, social, and political problems through cooperation in multilateral contexts.

I do not wish to conclude my discussion of multilateralism on a pessimistic note. But, I recently read a BBC article written in 2017 by Rachel Nuwer with the title, "How Western Civilization Could Collapse."[14] Although it has "Western civilization" in the title, the article actually talks about civilization as a whole. According to the article, there are four ways in which world civilization can collapse in the next half century. One way is by ecological strain and economic stratification. The ecological threat is the more widely understood and recognized path to potential doom, especially in terms of the depletion of natural resources exacerbated by climate change, although some major governments today do not acknowledge this. It could be that the world cannot solve the climate problem during this century, simply because it is more expensive in the short term to solve the problem than it is to just keep behaving as usual. The economic risk comes when elites push society toward instability and eventual collapse by hoarding huge quantities of wealth and resources and leaving little or none for commoners.

Finally, we can enter the danger zone through the increasing occurrence of "nonlinearities," or sudden, unexpected changes in the world's order, such as in Syria. In fact, unexpected changes in the world order have already begun to take place, as evidenced by the 2008 economic crisis, the rise of ISIS, Brexit, or Donald Trump's election in the United States. As people become more dissatisfied and afraid, they have a tendency to cling to their group identity, whether religious, racial or national. In other words, they become more parochial, less global, and

---

14   Rachel Nuwer, "How Western Civilisation Could Collapse," *BBC* (April, 2017)

To His Excellency Sung-joo Han
With best wishes,

Meeting President George W. Bush as a member of Korean presidential delegation to the
United States led by Hannara Party Chairman Chung Mong-joon, 2008

more unilateral.

However, let us not lose heart. Humanity and world civilization is not a lost cause. Using reason and science to guide decisions, paired with prudent leadership and good will, society can and should progress to higher and higher levels of well-being and development. Am I overly optimistic? Let us hope not.

Chapter 6

A Grand Strategy for South Korea?

During the course of my academic and foreign policy career, I inevitably had to think very carefully and deeply about the Republic of Korea (ROK)'s place in the world. While carrying out my duties from university professor to special representative to the U.N. Secretary-General, I was presented on many different occasions with the opportunity to think intensely and thoughtfully about South Korea's grand strategy. I was also forced to contemplate how such a grand strategy could most effectively be formulated and implemented. In this final chapter, I would like to share some of my knowledge and insight in the hopes that it will help future generations build a more secure and prosperous country and more fully contribute to the creation of a better global society.

All countries need a grand strategy. For the Republic of Korea, the nation's geopolitical position, the limits of its hard and soft power, and the division of the Korean Peninsula, make it very difficult to formulate a practical or feasible grand strategy. Under the current circumstances, South Korea is limited in the range of key strategic options it can pursue. Formulating a grand strategy and implementing it is a challenge for any country. Even countries that are more powerful and occupy a stronger geopolitical position may find their ability to implement a grand strategy to be limited. The reasons for this can be attributed to any of the following: strategic planners' limited ability to know and accurately predict events and circumstances; false reasoning on intellectual, ideological, or psychological grounds; goal displacement by institutions or regimes; unexpected or unplanned outcomes; and rejection of the grand strategy as a result of unanticipated needs and/or obstacles that arise.

In the spring and early summer of 2018, several events, including a summit meeting between South Korean President Moon Jae-in and North Korean leader Kim Jong-un followed by one between Kim and U.S. President Donald Trump, seem to place the Korean Peninsula at the crossroads of reconciliation and peace on the one hand and conflict and war on the other.

North Korea decided to participate in the 2018 Winter Olympics held in Pyeongchang, South Korea, and the South Korean government, led by Moon Jae-in, turned it into an opportunity to hold summit meetings between conflicting parties in South and North Korea, the United States, China, and Japan. They discussed denuclearization, inter-Korean cooperation and exchanges, conflict reduction, and peace. Given the peculiarities of the leaders involved and the divergent interests of various parties, the series of diplomatic maneuvers by the leaders required deep strategic thinking and tact.

The task is particularly formidable for South Korea, as it seeks to maintain peace and security, economic prosperity, and political independence. It must navigate through the rough waters of ambitious and powerful neighbors, all of which have competing national interests.

Despite the difficulties, it is clear that South Korea must continue to engage in deep strategic thinking for both the present and the future.

In this regard, creating long-term strategies is highly important. A broad survey of strategic issues shows that South Korea may not have much of a choice when it comes to maintaining its alliance with the United States, actively engaging and cooperating with the rest of the world, or pursuing a balanced policy of accommodation and assertiveness toward its neighbors. However, the country has a greater range of options on certain issues. For example, there is more flexibility in South Korea's strategy for dealing with the competitive relationship between the United States and China, its troubled relationship with Japan, or its relations with North Korea.

South Korea must continue to develop its strategic thinking, as the process of formulating and reassessing strategies will inevitably produce better policies. This, in turn, will earn South Korea respect and trust from other countries, build greater coherence and confidence in the country's actions, and help it to tackle larger tasks, such as unification. Finally, better strategic thinking will also contribute to greater understanding and unity among domestic constituencies within South Korea.

The Regional Landscape: South Korea and the Major Powers

The most pressing strategic issue for South Korea is how to position itself among the four most powerful nations in the region: the United States, China, Russia, and Japan. Therefore, to understand South Korea's strategic thinking, it is necessary to review the regional security landscape and several major developments that impact peace and security in Northeast Asia.

The first development is characterized by the rise of China and the emergence of what China describes as a "new type of major power relations." In other words, the geopolitical realities of the region, and the potential for conflict and cooperation, are highly influenced by two powers, the U.S. and China. With its growing economic power and military capabilities, China has begun to challenge the U.S.-dominated status quo and actively seeks to undermine parts of the international order that have existed since World War II. China seeks to reduce, if not end, the dominance of the U.S., especially in the Asian region. China is also determined to bring an end to U.S.-led alliances in Asia, which it considers Cold War relics. It has backed the establishment of the new Asian Infrastructure Investment Bank (AIIB) and has offered the countries in the region an alternative to infrastructure loans from the World Bank and Asian Development Bank (ADB). In effect, this directly challenges the power and influence of the U.S. in the fields of regional and international finance and banking. As a result, the conflict of interests between the U.S. and China is rapidly growing, and the two nations are increasingly in competition for regional influence, despite the need for cooperation in other aspects of their bilateral relations.

The second development is the growing tension and expansion of disputes between the U.S., on the one hand, and China and Russia on the other. This is exemplified by China's attempt to bring the South China Sea into its sphere of influence using confrontational tactics. China's actions included reclaiming land and building military facilities on Mischief Reef in the Spratly Islands, a move which faced strong opposition from the U.S., Japan, and neighboring Southeast Asian countries. The recent tensions with Russia have developed out of its actions in Ukraine. Russia's annexation of Crimea and military intervention in the Ukrainian conflict resulted in the imposition of economic sanctions against Russian individuals and companies by Western countries, to which Russia responded in kind.

A third major development is the warming of relations between China and Russia. Their growing disputes with the United States, and

Russia's increasing isolation from the West, have brought China and Russia closer together. The two countries have embarked on ambitious oil and gas deals together, and their newly reinvigorated relationship prompted Russia to sign an agreement promoting China's New Silk Road initiative, after an initial response that was lukewarm at best. They have also concluded a significant arms purchase agreement, enabling China to acquire large amounts of advanced military hardware from Russia. In this marriage of mutual convenience and needs, China seems to be getting the more advantageous end of the deal. Russia has committed to supplying China with low cost energy to meet its growing demands, and Beijing has also seized the opportunity to purchase weapons that make up some 60 percent of its arms imports.

Some observers argue that the simultaneous U.S. antagonism towards the two major world powers will push them to build a new political and military alignment, if not an alliance. But others assert that, because of the unequal nature of relations between Beijing and Moscow and the lack of trust between them, the chances of their forming a closer relationship are quite limited. Political scientist Joseph Nye, for example, recently stated that Russia is unlikely to be able to manage an alliance with China because "Russia's economic and military power has been in decline, whereas China's has exploded."[15]

Another reason precluding closer ties between China and Russia is the demographic imbalance between the sparsely populated Russian Far East and the densely populated Chinese territory across the border. A third factor that supposedly prevents closer ties is Russian unwillingness to become excessively dependent on China. Finally, experts argue that there is a fundamental lack of strategic trust and abundance of mutual suspicion, which will exclude the possibility of building a lasting

---

15   Joseph Nye, "A New Sino-Russian Alliance?". 2015. http://udenrigs.dk/new-sino-russian-alliance/

partnership.

Whatever the case may be with the Sino-Russian coalition, the continuing development of a stronger relationship will have a negative effect on the U.S.' ability to cooperate closely and productively with them in dealing with such critical issues as the North Korean nuclear and ballistic missiles threat. It will also affect the U.S.' ability to work with the two countries on trust-building and the establishment of a regional peace mechanism.

A fourth development that affects the regional situation is related to the evolving ambivalence of the U.S. policy toward Asia. The Obama administration characterized its policy towards the Asia-Pacific region as that of "rebalancing," which meant assigning a higher priority to political, economic, and security resources committed to the region. The main driver appeared to be the geopolitical realities of a rapidly rising China and the perceived need to respond. One of the fundamental elements of the policy was to strengthen relationships with allies and partners, including emerging powers such as India and Indonesia. These strategic plans were being implemented even as the U.S. continued to tighten its military budget.

However, many of the tenets of the former "rebalancing" strategy are being called into question by the new Trump administration in the United States. In the midst of the growing tension and competition in the region, the presidency in the U.S. of Donald Trump, a self-styled deal maker and provocateur of other countries, friends and foes alike, in the name of "America first policy" has made it more difficult and complicated for a country like South Korea which is heavily dependent on the United States for security and international economic relations to cope with the changes to the global security environment. While the tension between U.S. isolationism and internationalism is not new, countries like South Korea with historically close relations with the United States find themselves in uncertain territory for the first time in many years. The reason is that, during the first two years of his presidency, President Donald Trump has shown to be a leader who tends to rip up international norms and defy common expectations and predictability, bringing a new equation into the international and regional order. Trump has threatened to tear up trade agreements and impose trade tariffs on traditional allies such as Canada, Germany and France. At the same time he has also threatened to demand that other allied countries pay more for the stationing of U.S. troops on their territories.

Paradoxically, while Trump himself has questioned the value of U.S. alliance relationships around the world, the administration has also been strengthening its alliances with Australia, Japan, and South Korea. It has assigned more resources to the region because of the perceived dynamism, opportunities, and challenges. The Trump government has begun to bring India into the coalition, emphasizing its new "Indo-Pacific strategy." The policy has attempted, with some success, to embed the United States in the emerging political, security, and economic architecture, including the East Asia Summit (EAS) and strengthen linkages of the U.S.-Pacific-Indian Ocean crescent. The policy even seeks to establish a more extensive and structured relationship with ASEAN.

At the same time, rather than focusing on the containment of China, the U.S. has tried, with limited success, to maintain a positive and stable relationship with Beijing. A strategic policy that furthers cooperation and manages tensions in this bilateral relationship has been seen as more favorable than one that fosters competition and conflict. In the course of implementing its new Asia policy, the U.S. has also been forced to turn its attention away from the region and expend energy elsewhere, such as the Middle East and Europe. Subsequently, the continuing troubles in these regions have made it difficult for the U.S. to pivot away.

The potential emerging trade war with China, however, could complicate regional dynamics considerably in the near future. The pivot to Asia policy has also encountered difficulties due to China's suspicions of U.S. intentions. China believes the real U.S. objective is to maintain its position of supremacy in Asia and contain China. Russia has also reacted to the U.S. policy by "turning to," if not "rebalancing to," the Northeast Asian region. Russia must also deal with a rising China seeking to impose its will on territorial issues, and intensifying maritime and territorial disputes in the East and South China Seas. Moscow sees Beijing as being prepared to use its growing economic leverage to counter America and expand its own sphere of influence.

A number of China's neighbors likewise see the country's rising power as a threat and believe that China will utilize its military to enforce its territorial claims. They worry that China will use its economic leverage to diminish their response options, and so they have sought out America's reassurance and support. This, in turn, has persuaded Beijing that the U.S. is orchestrating a plan to create increased regional opposition toward China in order to isolate and contain the country.

With regards to Japan, the U.S. is closely cooperating with Prime Minister Abe's government to implement its Asia policy. Japan has revised the interpretation of its Peace Constitution to make "collective self-defense" possible. The government has agreed on new "defense guidelines," enacted through legislation in the National Diet, which will allow the use of Japanese forces beyond the defense of the archipelago proper. The new U.S.–Japan Defense Guidelines adopted in April 2015 state that the Self-Defense Forces will conduct appropriate operations involving the use of force to respond to situations where an armed attack against a foreign country that is in a close relationship with Japan occurs. Japan is also collaborating closely on a ballistic missile defense (BMD) project, and it has been working in tandem with the U.S. to denounce China's territorial expansion schemes in the South China Sea.

The United States regards Japan as a much more willing partner to deal with disputes with China than its other close regional ally, South Korea. This is because South Korea takes a somewhat less confrontational approach towards China. Even though South Korea has also been strengthening its alliance with the U.S. on a range of issues, it has taken a more circumspect approach than Japan in disputes between the United States and China for several understandable reasons.

First, as a divided country facing the North Korean threat of conventional weapons and weapons of mass destruction (WMDs), South Korea regards China as a key country with which it must actively pursue coordination. Second, it wishes to find the most effective and pragmatic way to deal with the Chinese challenge without unnecessarily and excessively antagonizing Beijing. Third, because of the enormous economic interdependence with China, South Korea is much more vulnerable to Chinese economic pressure than Japan is. Finally, it believes that the best way to maintain peace, harmony, and cooperation in the region is to find common ground and interests, to engage in dialogue and trust-building, and to diminish mutual suspicions and harsh rhetoric.

The United States, from its perspective, has a distinct need to maintain closely coordinated alliance relationships with both Korea and Japan to counter China's rising power and the North Korean threat. At the same time, it must acknowledge and respect each country's policies towards China and North Korea. This makes it difficult to carry out a comprehensive "rebalancing" policy and often strains relations among the three countries.

Recent efforts, in the first half of 2018, to reengage North Korea in a diplomatic process to dismantle its nuclear weapons program have also complicated the regional picture and U.S. involvement in the Asia-

Pacific. In the wake of the "Singapore summit" between Donald Trump and Kim Jong-un on June 12th, the United States seems to be trying to bring North Korea into its fold with a higher dose of carrots in the balance between rewards for good behavior and punishments for bad behavior. It remains to be seen how this process will play out.

Turning back to the larger strategic picture in the region, a fifth development has to do with the troubled and deteriorating relationship between Japan and Korea. Close neighbors, the two throughout history have had a checkered relationship of competition, cooperation, and occupation. The most recent example of this troublesome past was the Japanese colonial domination of Korea for 35 years in the first half of the twentieth century. Seventy years after the end of World War II and Korea's liberation from Japanese occupation, they have yet to throw off the shackles of the past and move beyond the legacies of pervious historical misdeeds and grievances.

In particular, the two countries still dispute the factual record of "comfort women," or those young women who were forced into sexual slavery by the Imperial Japanese Army in the occupied territories before and during World War II. Seoul and Tokyo still have not agreed on a permanent resolution to this dispute because they are unable to find a satisfactory method for compensating the comfort women victims. There have been previous attempts, but Japan complains that Koreans are never satisfied with Japanese apologies and keep moving the goalpost for a final resolution. Koreans complain that Japanese apologies are never sincere or sufficient and that Japanese leaders keep making statements that are offensive to and dismissive of Koreans.

From the U.S. standpoint, quarrels between its two Asian allies are a vexing problem, adversely affecting the collaboration not only between them, but among all three countries. It also tends to make Korea and China strange bedfellows, both of which have unsettled grievances toward Japan.

It has been more than 50 years since Korea and Japan normalized their diplomatic relations. There is still hope in both countries that Koreans will adopt a more generous and magnanimous frame of mind to forgive past historical misdeeds, and the Japanese will undertake a more sincere and deeper reflection of the past and present a way to resolve the issue of accountability. If this happens, the two countries may finally be able to establish common ground for greater understanding, cooperation, and lasting friendship.

Finally, North Korea's nuclear program still presents a peculiar dilemma to South Korea and its neighbors. The intractable nature of the North Korean problem and continued nuclear and ballistic missile provocations over the last several years had led to a palpable sense of fatigue and resignation among the countries to the Six-Party Talks. Under the leadership of Kim Jong-un, North Korea has not only codified in the preamble of its constitution that the DPRK is a nuclear weapons state, but it also officially adopted a *byungjin* (two-track) policy for simultaneous development of nuclear weapons and the economy. While there has been a brief respite from North Korean missile tests over the last few months due to ongoing dialogue between the two Koreas and the U.S. and North Korea, it is unclear how far the negotiations process will take us. It is also unclear if Kim Jong-un will pivot away from the *byungjin* policy toward a policy of true economic development and internal reform. Despite the display of North Korean gestures of possible accommodation as shown in the "signed agreement" at the Trump-Kim meeting in Singapore, North Korea shows no signs of slowing down, much less dismantling its nuclear and missile capabilities. Even as President Trump attempts to construe the meeting as major progress toward North Korean denuclearization, the announced results do not indicate any likelihood nor certainty that North Korea will indeed denuclearize itself within a given time frame.

Thus, in addition to potential ongoing diplomacy with North Korea in the remaining half of 2018, the United States and other countries in the region should seriously seek to reexamine their strategies for deterring and containing the North Korean threat, and rolling back the North Korean nuclear program in earnest. Failing to limit the DPRK's nuclear development now means that its program will only get exponentially more dangerous in the years to come.

It has been a quarter century since the Cold War ended. East Asia has moved from a period when international relations were primarily dominated by the U.S.-Soviet bipolar power structure to a unipolar situation in which the United States maintained control over the region through its hegemonic position. Recent years have brought about another shift, which can be described as an emerging G2 structure, plus an evolving balance of power. East Asia today has a situation in which the continental powers of China and Russia are on one side, and the United States and Japan, essentially maritime powers, are on the other. South Korea has been leaning heavily towards the maritime coalition, and North Korea remains isolated, but leaning towards the continental powers. However, this divide is not like the one the world experienced during the Cold War. There is still time to seek cooperation among all the powers on a range of issues and create a regional architecture for peace, security, and prosperity. It would be in Korea's interest if trust can be built not only between the United States and China, but also between Russia and the United States, Japan and China, Japan and Korea, between the two Koreas and even between the United States and North Korea. All these actors are heavily interdependent on one another economically, a fact which both necessitates and enables countries to seek cooperation and peace in the region.

Strategic Choices

Where does the newly emerging regional security landscape leave South Korea? What role can and should it play? The following is a summary of the various strategic options that South Korea may pursue, split into eight different threads, in some cases with overlapping and conflicting policy prescriptions.

1. Tilting: Because Korea is a peninsular country, there has been a debate as to whether its course should be that of a continental or a maritime power. Leaning towards becoming a maritime country would mean aligning itself more closely with the United States and Japan, whereas identifying itself as a continental power would mean placing greater emphasis on relations with China and Russia. Given the need to maintain amicable relations with all four, tilting is neither realistic nor practical.

2. Balancer: Roh Moo-hyun, president from 2003 to 2008, advocated that Korea be the regional balancer between China and Japan, a role somewhat akin to that which the United Kingdom played in the European balance of power in the eighteenth and nineteenth centuries. This policy was criticized at home as being unrealistic and pretentious, but it reflected the growing sense of self-confidence in a more assertive Korean nation and the desire to reclaim ownership of foreign relations.

3. Equidistance: This is a policy that is similar to that of a balancer, except that it does not call for Korea to "tilt" in either direction on regional issues in order to keep regional relations balanced. Given the multiplicity of issues that require joining forces with one nation or the other, this strategy may be impractical for Korea to pursue in any consistent and meaningful way.

4. Hedging: This is a policy of cultivating a fallback position and ultimately going with the prospective winner. Hedging is more dynamic

and flexible than maintaining a balance or keeping equidistance between countries. As such, it could be seen by friends and adversaries alike as being opportunistic, unreliable, and untrustworthy. It is a strategy that is likely to subject the country to greater pressure from outside powers. One example of this is when South Korea adopted a policy of "strategic ambiguity" on Terminal High Altitude Area Defense (THAAD). The only possible advantage of a hedging strategy would be that the country does not need to be tied to a particular power or group of countries and, thus, would retain a degree of flexibility and freedom of choice. But the cost of flexibility far outweighs its benefits.

5. Bridge: This is a policy based on the assumption that Northeast Asian countries should minimize conflict and maximize cooperation, and that Korea could be a harmonizer among the major powers. Since Korea is situated between the major powers not only geographically, but also in economic development, temperament, and culture, the proponents of this strategy will argue that Korea can play a bridging role among the powers. However, given the large gap in interests and objectives of the powers, there are limits to the bridging role that Korea could play, even if it chooses to do so.

6. Equal Competitor: This is a policy predicated upon the belief that South Korea has reached a level where it can stand alongside its neighbors and deal with them as equals. It does not assume that Korea is indeed equal in economic prowess, diplomatic clout, or population, but argues that Korea's growth has now put it at a level where it is not a "shrimp amid whales." The argument for this policy is also a reflection of growing Korean self-confidence and self-esteem.

7. Community: This policy is based on the belief that the three Northeast Asian nations have enough shared interests and commonalities that they can form a community. Community-building can start with integration and cooperation in economics (a three-country free trade

agreement, for example), the environment, and cultural exchanges. Such a community could be built on the shared culture and common interests of the countries of the region.

8. Status Quo (Balance of Power): According to this view, the current situation in which South Korea and Japan are allied with the United States, and China is aligned with Russia and supportive of North Korea, is an acceptable power configuration in Northeast Asia, even if not the most preferable one. In this configuration, China maintains strong economic relations not only with the United States but also with Japan and South Korea. This view assumes that while China remains South Korea's largest trading partner, the ROK will stay closely tied to the United States and Japan for security and political relations. It also assumes that even as China's economic and military power grows, its economic interdependence with other countries will continue to dictate a cooperative Chinese policy with the other Northeast Asian states.

Conclusion

The above review of South Korea's strategic options shows that the country may have a range of choices when it comes to determining policy in different issue areas. When examining strategy in the context of the broader regional security landscape, however, the picture becomes less clear. One can see that the formulation of a grand strategy is nearly impossible because South Korea's different policy prescriptions are extremely difficult to establish and maintain. None of the choices are exhaustive, mutually exclusive, or permanent. The United States, China, South Korea, and Japan have different interests in and perspectives on a range of issues, but that should not prevent South Korea from pursuing the development of strategic thoughts and plans. The policy options discussed above are possible choices, but South Korea does not need to choose only one right now. Rather, it is important to think about and discuss when, in what sequence, in what combination, and which strategic option(s) to choose. In order to survive, navigate, and thrive in this turbulent neighborhood, Korea will have to adopt varying mixtures of the above alternatives according to the needs and dictates of time and circumstances. This should drive strategic thinkers in South Korea and other countries in the region to diligently create new options or to reassess those strategies already in place. The increased reliability and consistency of policies formulated out of this strategic thought process will lead to greater trust building and cooperation among countries in the region.

As important as which strategic option(s) to choose is in what way and to what extent the strategy is formulated and how the policies are pursued. A strategy needs constancy without being rigid, flexibility without being void of direction, and thoroughness without being extreme. The leaders creating such strategies and policies should have convictions and principles but need to remain open to communication and opposing views.

Afterword

Koreans are used to being on the brink of both war and peace, although war often seems more imminent than peace. Sometimes a devastating war does take place. Other times they avoid it, by luck, fortitude, or skillful maneuvering (i.e., diplomacy). Yet, even when war occurs, they somehow recover from the devastation and maintain their identity, as they did after the Korean War of 1950-53. This is why Koreans have sayings like, "Even if heaven tumbles down, there's always a hole to soar through." This is also probably why, to foreigners who observe them, Koreans seem surprisingly sanguine, if not nonchalant, in the face of missile and artillery threats from only 40 kilometers north of Seoul, where more than 10 million people live.

South Koreans disagree a lot about important questions: How great is the danger to the country at any given time? Who are our enemies and who are our friends? How benign or malignant are our adversaries' intentions? What to do about the dangers all around us? How can we make, secure, and build peace? Regardless, to survive and thrive, separately or together, we need skillful and robust diplomacy.

But just as Korea has serious and difficult diplomatic challenges, its ability to conduct effective diplomacy is limited by the circumstances in the region and conditions of their own making. Korea is a divided country between the North and the South, who in the last century fought a devastating internecine war, despite sharing the same ethnicity,

Visiting Mt. Baekdusan's Chonji with wife Song-mi, 2002

language, and culture. Although there are occasional charades of peace and reconciliation, they are armed against each other and are still at each other's throats as proxies of more powerful outside powers.

I have learned three things from the experience of handling diplomacy during a period when the country was on the brink of war: 1) We need to think pragmatically, free from time-worn ideology, emotions born of historical legacy, and domestic political constraints in order to work towards consensus and bipartisanship; 2) We need balanced thinking—it is possible to be proud and independent-minded, but we also need to be able to compromise and accommodate when the time comes; and 3) We need to be realistic and smart, recognizing that we cannot deal with challenges with courage and ardor alone.

In Korea, it is customary to say in your thank-you note at the end of your tenure as a government official that you are grateful to your colleagues for their help so that "no major mishap happened during my tenure." I used to think that that was much too modest and conceited a goal for a responsible official. At the same time, one does realize how lucky one is if he or she could leave office without a major mishap. Is it because disasters and mishaps happen so often in Korea, or because they were averted by your able and astute stewardship?

Ultimately, I think it has to do with the timing of one's service. But what one does and how one performs his or her duties do matter. And, in turn, this is related to how one approaches problems and challenges and makes the best use of the opportunities and resources that are available.

Inspecting "Green Line" in Cyprus, August, 1996

About the Author

Han SungJoo is a Professor Emeritus at Korea University. Prof. Han previously served as the Minister of Foreign Affairs (1993-1994), UN Secretary-General's Special Representative for Cyprus (1996-1997), a member of the UN Inquiry Commission on the 1994 Rwanda Genocide (1999), Chairman of the East Asia Vision Group (2000-2001), Ambassador of the Republic of Korea to the United States (2003-2005), and Acting President of Korea University(2002, 2006-2007)

Prof. Han is a graduate of Seoul National University (1962) and received a Ph.D. in Political Science from the University of California, Berkeley (1970). Previously, he taught at City University of New York (1970-1978) and was a visiting Professor at Columbia University (1986-1987) and Stanford University (1992, 1995). He was also a Distinguished Fellow at the Rockefeller Brothers Fund (1986-1987).

He frequently played a consulting role for the Korean government, including several presidents, the ministry of foreign affairs, ministry of national defense, and ministry of national unification. He is also a chair professor at the National Diplomatic Academy of Korea.

His English publications include *Korean Diplomacy in an Era of Globalization* (1995), *Korea in a Changing World* (1995), and *Changing Values in Asia* (1999). He has many publications in Korean, including *Nam Gwa Puk, kurigo Sekye* (The Two Koreas and the World) (2000), and most recently a memoir in Korean, *Oegyoui Gil* (My Diplomatic Journey) (2017).

Peace-Building with Former US Secretary of Defense William Perry, Stanford, 2005

INDEX